Writing in English

Book 2

Anita Pincas
with the assistance of
Barbara Johnson
and Kate Allen

First published 1982
Reprinted 1983, 1984 (twice), 1985, 1986, 1987, 1988, 1989, 1991

Published by *Macmillan Publishers Ltd*
London and Basingstoke

ISBN 0 333 31762 9

Printed in Hong Kong

Acknowledgements

The Author and Publishers wish to acknowledge with thanks the following photographic sources, and to state that they have tried to contact all copyright holders but in any case where they may have failed, will be pleased to make the necessary arrangement at the first opportunity.

Barnabys Picture Library
British Hovercraft
British Tourist Authority
French Tourist Board
Japanese Embassy
Japan National Tourist Organization
The Mansell Collection
Massey-Ferguson (UK) Ltd
Museum of English Rural Life
National Portrait Gallery
National Savings
Popperfoto
Zbigniew Ropek
Shell/Esso
Simon of Newbury
South East England Tourist Board
John Topham Picture Library
UNICEF
UPI
The Welsh Guards
The Yugoslavia Tourist Board

Contents

Teacher's notes

Based on *Teaching English writing* by Anita Pincas (Macmillan, 1982)

1 A brief introduction to the teaching of writing Writing is an instrument of both communication and self-expression. Most people, however, especially when writing in a foreign or second language, use it primarily to communicate with other members of their own community or the wider world. Our main task is therefore to teach effective functional writing rather than creative self-expression. There are a few initial guiding principles to note:

1 Writing should be as close as possible to genuine functional use of language, as opposed to the traditional set-piece classroom composition for the eyes of the teacher only.

2 Since people's ways of communicating information are very varied, there is no single way of writing correct English. It is therefore important for students to read as widely as possible in order to become familiar with different varieties of written English. They cannot be expected to write in a style which they have never seen or read.

3 Good writing depends on a set of specific writing skills. It does not follow automatically from good grammar and adequate vocabulary.

This book and the other two in this series cover a wide range of functional types of writing. But it is assumed that the practice will be done as part of a normal language course in which students are reading an adequate amount. It is hoped that teachers will supplement the work in each unit by bringing into the classroom as much sample material of written English as they can get hold of, eg English passports, letters, newspaper cuttings, magazine advertisements, official forms and leaflets, posters, etc, in addition to traditional essays and stories.

As far as writing skills are concerned, they can be grouped in three main areas:

I Communicative skills: making the writing functional, ie fulfilling a specific purpose and suiting a specific subject-matter. For more details, see *Teaching English Writing* Chapter 2.

II Organisational skills: organising ideas, constructing paragraphs, and using linking words. For more details, see *Teaching English Writing* Chapter 3.

III Stylistic skills: handling the four major styles (narrative, descriptive, expository, and argumentative), and achieving the right level of formality and the appropriate tone. For more details, see *Teaching English Writing* Chapter 4.

The three books in the *Writing in English* series deal with all these skills. Book 1 places emphasis on those areas that relate most easily to elementary grammar and vocabulary. Subject-matter is not too complex for the language available (though it is not childish), and paragraphs are kept short. Narrative has been given some space, but description, exposition and argument are given equal weight. Books 2 and 3 then continue to build up competence in the various writing skills with gradually increasing maturity of English.

2 Grading The grading of the three books is as follows:

Book I: Vocabulary is limited to the 1800 headwords in *A Learner's First Dictionary* (Macmillan) which is based on criteria of practicality and frequency, and includes all items from the Council of Europe's 'Threshold' syllabus. (For the very few words that go beyond this dictionary, help is usually given by the illustrations, but students should in any case be encouraged to use a native-language/English dictionary.) Structures are limited to those in Stages 1 and 2 of *English Grammatical Structure* by L.G. Alexander *et al*, (Longman, 1975), though not all structures listed there actually appear in the book. As a writing book, *Writing in English* does not aim to practise structures. However the Table of Contents indicates the main structures relevant to each unit, and teachers could therefore usefully link structure drills with the writing practice.

Book II: Vocabulary is limited to the 4,700 headwords and derivatives in the Macmillan *New Basic Dictionary*, based on a selection from current lexical surveys and conforming with the Council of Europe recommendations. Structures are limited to those up to Stage 4 in *English Grammatical Structure* (see above).

Book III: Vocabulary is not limited, and students should be competent in using a dictionary by this stage. Structures are limited to those up to Stage 5 in *English Grammatical Structure* (see above).

In all three books, the units follow on from each other and should be used in the order given. There are revision units at regular intervals.

It is impossible to lay down fixed recommendations about when writing work of this kind should be started. Different educational systems have different requirements and policies, and what might be appropriate in the first year of English in one system might be relevant only for the second or third year in another. It can be said quite unequivocally, however, that as soon as students can handle the level of English in *Writing in English I* they should start writing paragraphs and whole pieces of written English, ie they should move beyond the isolated sentences of their structure drills. Only when they do this are they attempting to use the language in a genuine way.

3 Using this book All units after 1 and 2 (which establish the basic concept of the paragraph) follow roughly the same plan. The first one or two exercises help to familarise students with the kind of writing to be practised. The next exercises are fairly controlled while the final one is fairly free and is usually either to be done in a group or as part of a game.

Exercises are of well-known types — completion, sentence combining, completing frames, re-ordering mixed sentences, etc. But they are not designed to practise vocabulary or structures. They highlight specific writing skills such as the use of linking words, spatial description, lay-out of letters, etc.

In addition, there are numerous examples of different kinds of paragraphs, and plans to help students construct their own.

The use of group work (which includes writing games) might at first sight appear inappropriate for the teaching of writing. In general, however, *group work* means that there is some kind of cooperation between the members of the class, who are divided into conveniently-sized groups for the purpose. They might be discussing something in pairs before starting to write; they might play a game involving two teams; they might write a letter that another student will have to read and answer; or they might split responsibility among different students so that one student collects information, another organises it and a third actually writes whatever has to be written. Even when group work is not explicitly mentioned in the exercises, teachers should encourage it wherever possible. (Conversely, most exercises that are set up for group activity in Book I can be used for individual work if necessary.)

Moreover, group work can go beyond preparation for writing. The members of a pair, or larger group, can actually *do the writing together*. They can discuss the exact words and sentences to be used, and then either each student writes down what was said, or else they appoint one member of the group to be the writer for all of them. It is always important for the teacher to move fairly systematically around the room, helping each group with vocabulary, making sure everyone is involved, but not staying too long with any group since the main initiative for writing should rest with the students.

Group activity has two practical benefits in the teaching of writing. Firstly, it overcomes the boredom and frequent frustration of traditional methods where each student is sitting silently at his desk, racking his brains for something to write. Secondly, it provides a situation in which students have to communicate with each other, both in speech and writing. Students are then writing for a real reader, not just for the critical eyes of the teacher. Having a real reader will help them to see their writing from the point of view of the person who receives it — they will be forced to consider whether it is clear enough and will soon discover whether it was successful or not for the purpose of the activity.

As for games, needless to say they should be lively and enjoyable. This means that students should not be too much inhibited by the fear of making mistakes. Teachers will find that adults quickly adapt to games as long as their purpose in the writing lesson is clear and they do not overshadow what the students feel to be their main objectives. For more discussion of games see *Teaching techniques in communicative English* (J. Revell, 1982), and *How to use games in language teaching* (S. Rixon, 1982). Both are in the Macmillan Essential Language Teaching Series, Ed. R.H. Flavell.

There is further discussion of teaching methods for familiarisation, controlled/guided and free writing, in *Teaching English writing* Chapters 1, 5, 6, 7 and 8. See particularly Chapter 5 which offers a blueprint for the preparation of further exercises.

4 Notes on individual units Before teaching any unit, teachers should check the list of *Main Structures* in the Contents chart and set up some preparatory drills if necessary. The list does not give all the structures in a unit, only the main ones required for the exercises.

The units have been written as a developing sequence, with regular revision and reference back to previous units. They must be worked in the order given.

At early stages, especially, the teacher should accept and make clear to the students that a lot of the work is preparatory and will lead to more realistic writing later. For instance, some of the letters in Book 1 are simple versions of what an English person would really write, but they are acceptable at this level.

The notes on *further work* are particularly important since, within the confines of this book, it is impossible to include as much writing practice as students really need. Sometimes the further work lends itself to homework, sometimes to classroom activity. Teachers should think of it as part of each unit, though of course they can substitute something different if necessary. In all the exercises, but perhaps most in the *further work*, teachers will have to make decisions about how much error to allow uncorrected. Current opinion is that only errors related to the teaching aim of the exercise should be remarked upon. See *Language learners and their errors* (J.A. Norrish, 1982) in the Macmillan Essential Language Teaching Series.

Unit 1

This unit practises very straightforward narrative in chronological order. It emphasises the use of linking words. (These are discussed in Chapter 3 of *Teaching English writing*.) *First* and *finally* are obviously in a fixed position, but the others could change places. Students should be careful not to use a series of sentences all starting with the same linking word, eg *then*. Two in succession is the maximum that should be allowed. The unit also requires the past tense form of the irregular verbs: *be, cut, marry, find, give, put, die, have, send, wake, hurry, drive, run, see, steal, take, write, eat*.

Further work Students probably know events in the history of their country that could be similarly described in chronological order with the same linking words. They can get information from history books in their own language if necessary.

Unit 2

The general aim is to write clear and logical descriptions contrasting two things. Two kinds of linking devices are used: (a) *it* and *one(s)* to refer back to something already mentioned, and (b) *but, however*, and *on the other hand*, which mean substantially the same thing, but the first normally occurs within a sentence while the other two can start a sentence. Completion exercise 1(i) highlights both the logical arrangement of contrasting descriptions and the use of these linking devices. The essay plan in Exercise 4 shows the same logical arrangement. The students' description in Exercise 5(ii) should follow this arrangement if possible.

Further work Some examples of *however* and *on the other hand* in other positions in sentences could be demonstrated:

John, | however, / on the other hand, | will stay at home.

John will stay at home, | however. / on the other hand.

Letters similar to those used in the unit can deal with other choices, eg choosing a college for future study, choosing a sports club, a band to play music for a party, a camera, etc. If vocabulary for these topics is lacking, students must be taught how to use a good dictionary.

Unit 3

Places are here described in a very general way, ie there is no detailed description but rather a series of salient features arranged systematically — in this case under three headings: natural beauty, sport, theatres. There are three major linking devices: *for example* introduces one or more examples of something said in the immediately preceding sentence or clause; *in addition* introduces further information about a topic; *besides this* introduces new information of a different kind. The first can occur in positions other than initial:

You can, *for example*, ski in the mountains.
You can ski in the mountains, *for example*.

Exercise 3 adds the element of contrast to the description. The correct choices in the paragraph are: *for example, on the other hand*, and *besides this*.

Further work Exercise 5 asks for a paragraph like the one in Exercise 3 or the one in Exercise 4. Students could, however, use the first three paragraphs in Exercise 1 as a model to write about a country they know well. The general pattern of these three paragraphs can be extended to descriptions of other places, eg a college, a holiday resort, or to describe the skills and character of a person.

Unit 4

This unit brings together some of the aspects of the preceding units on narrative, description, and comparison. Exercise 1 should arouse interest in the general question of measuring personality which is continued in Exercise 2, and the writing in Exercises 3 and 4 then requires the linking words introduced in Units 2 and 3. Exercise 5 uses the linking words introduced in Unit 1.

Further work Students might like to write about themselves, contrasting the characteristics they possess with those they would like to have. To do this they would need structures like 'but I would like to be ....' or 'I would rather be ....' or 'I wish, however, that I were/had ....'. Another way of writing about themselves is to compare their own personality with that of someone they particularly admire.

Unit 5

More linking words are introduced, but the main objective is to exemplify three different paragraphs, one for each stage of a narrative. Paragraphing is crucial to good writing, but there are no simple rules. It is partly a matter of logic, partly a matter of emphasis (short paragraphs tend to highlight main points). For a discussion of paragraphs, see Chapter 3 of *Teaching English Writing*.

Further work Students could write about another topic, not necessarily a narrative, that falls conveniently into three parts, perhaps related to history or to a science experiment they have done. It is always helpful to relate writing to their interests outside the classroom!

Unit 6

This unit shows two usages that contrast with the conventional 'complete sentences' of formal written English: the language of note-taking, and the shortened sentences of normal speech. Note-taking is a skill that many students may need. The exercises emphasise the importance of organising notes under topic headings. Shortened sentences, on the other hand, are not really necessary for communication though they make speech sound more natural. They are included here because students will encounter them in reading or on the radio, and they should have some idea of this important difference between speech and writing. Some of the shortened forms may look a little strange written down ('Always notice hands.') but when spoken at conversation speed they sound quite normal.

Further work Students can practise taking notes while somebody speaks. The teacher or another student could report a football match or other event they have recently seen, while the class takes notes. They then divide into small groups and write a report using their notes. For group work like this, either each student writes the whole report after discussion with the group or else the group appoints one person to be the 'writer' for all of them.

An amusing game to play is as follows: The day after this unit has been done, the teacher (without having warned the class) comes into the room for the lesson and for about five minutes does a number of unusual things (eg puts a large suitcase on the desk, places a cake under the chair, etc.). He offers no explanation of what he is doing. When he has finished, he says he wants to test their powers of observation, or their memory, and asks them to write as exact a report as they can of what he did. The game thus practises reporting observed actions.

Unit 7

Two kinds of tabulation present information for writing: a summary of travel options and an itinerary. Reading such tabulations is an important skill, and students would do well also to learn to write them, as part of summarising or essay-planning.

Possibility is expressed in two ways in the unit. The first, *can*, here indicates the speaker's certainty about his description of the possibilites. The second, *may*, here indicates that he is less certain. 'You can go . . .', means 'It is possible for you to go ...' but 'You may want to . . .' means 'Perhaps you want to . . .'. In Exercise 4 'we can meet you' means 'it is possible for us to meet you', while 'we may be able to share the cost' means 'perhaps we will be able to share the cost'.

The use of *alternatively* is very similar to *on the other hand*, but is restricted to contexts where two alternatives are being considered. *On the other hand* can be used simply to introduce a different idea into a discussion.

The *if* conditional is the simple *if* + present tense followed by future tense in the next clause. It may, at first sight, look more complex here because of the *will have to* construction.

Notice the special use of the present tense in Exercise 3. All the verbs of travel (*fly, take, continue*) are in the simple present, though it would be equally correct to use the future. However, the use illustrated in this paragraph is typical of plans for future actions. The *will* future in this paragraph refers to continuous periods of time, ie *will stay* and *will spend*.

For Exercises 4 and 5 it would be useful to have a map available.

Further work Other topics related to future plans could lead to similar writing, eg planning a series of sports matches which involve getting different teams together, or a series of political meetings, or in a business context some committee meetings that involve staff from different departments. In each case, times and dates and places have to be proposed and then suggestions have to be made to fit everybody in. In the unit, only two sets of people have to meet, but the writing would become more complex if three or more were involved.

The work would proceed as follows: Students imagine a group at a college who wish to start a drama club. They have written to the Head asking for permission to use some college rooms and he replied with a letter and chart very similar to those in Exercise 1, suggesting two or three possibilities. Students write the chart and the Head's letter, indicating which rooms are available for use, what days of the week they are available and how many people can fit in.

Then students move on to writing as in Exercise 3. They prepare the equivalent of an itinerary, ie a list of dates, times and rooms chosen, and write a paragraph similar to that in Exercise 3. Finally, they imagine that another club, eg the music club, would like combined meetings with the drama club but is restricted in the times they can come. Students work out when and where the two clubs can get together and write a letter making suggestions as in Exercise 4.

Unit 8

The re-ordering exercise highlights logical arrangement of sentences within paragraphs as well as certain linking devices that signal which sentences go in sequence. For example, to deal with sentences numbered 3, 5, 9, and 14, it is necessary to work out what preceding sentences the *he* could refer back to; sentence 4, containing the word *different* relates back to sentence 2 which also has that word; there are parallel ideas between sentences 5 and 7, or 8 and 13, so these may follow each other. However, as indicated in Exercise 2, there are at least two ways of arranging the sentences. If students have too much difficulty with Exercise 1, they should refer to the plans in Exercise 2 and follow one or the other. The letter to be written in Exercise 2(ii) could be a fairly straightforward 'copy' of the original with only the persons changed, ie all references to Richard become 'I', and all 'I's become references to the cousin who has to be given a name.

The story in Exercises 4 and 5 will not involve comparison as in the earlier exercises, but the aim is that students should plan it before they write and try to group sentences into paragraphs in a logical way.

Further work Writing similar to that in the first three exercises could compare two people's different experiences at a party, during college studies, during their early life, during the first year of marriage, etc. Re-ordering exercises are best prepared from professionally written stories. Each sentence is written on a separate slip of paper, and the pieces are re-arranged at random. The length of Exercise 1 is about the maximum that most students could deal with.

For story-writing, it is interesting to let students finish off a story of which they are given only the beginning, or the end, or the middle, and then compare what they have done with the original. Stories chosen for this could be published work or the students' own efforts.

Unit 9

This unit emphasises reported speech as well as essay planning. In Exercise 3 the plan for the letter is in fact given by the posture chart, which classifies the various aspects of posture in five groups. Students could take a new paragraph for each group, or combine the two groups related to 'working' and the two related to 'sitting' and 'lying down'.

Reported speech should be revised before this unit, especially constructions like 'he advised me to ...' compared with 'he warned me that ...'.

Further work Letters reporting advice given to the writer can be continued on subjects close to students' interests. However, writing done by students need not always be prose. They could prepare a chart similar to the posture chart, with simple stick drawings and simple instructions. The chart could classify the main aspects of a skill that they know very well, for instance driving a car, riding a bicycle, playing a sport, playing a musical instrument, etc.

The style of English in Exercise 1 could be a model for similar messages coming from, say, an army patrol to base, a group of mountain climbers to a rescue team, a group of explorers to a distant town, a team of scientists travelling across the Antarctic to their base, or a spaceship to earth.

Unit 10

Students will, of course, be familiar with advertisements in their own language, and this unit could profitably be introduced by a critical discussion of the language and persuasive devices used by the advertising industry. The chief techniques to note are: (a) attempts to avoid giving real facts, (b) the use of words to create a pleasant and favourable mood, and (c) illustrations that emphasise the product's best features. In Exercise 5 students could try to write both an 'honest' and a 'dishonest' advertisement.

Further work Methods of persuasion are, of course, not limited to advertising. Students could look at political slogans and political literature for instance. Many popular songs, especially by the Beatles, are persuasive, relying on emotive impressions rather than a genuine, factual argument.

Unit 11

Adjectives and adverbs are relevant to the previous unit on persuasive writing, but in this unit they are dealt with from a grammatical viewpoint. The order suggested in the tables in Exercises 1 and 4 is not an absolute rule, but it is a safe guideline for learners. The important point of the exercises, however, is to give examples of why such strings might be appropriate in writing. The reason in these examples is to compress information that would otherwise occur in a series of simple sentences (often found in student essays!)

Further work The exercises can be repeated with different subject-matter. For instance, other items can be listed on an insurance claim-form — personal effects, sports equipment, photographic equipment, etc. Instead of purchases and instructions for first aid, students could do similar writing for preparation of a science experiment, a botanical field trip, a party, cooking a meal, or the skill they may have already dealt with in Unit 9 (see Further Work for that unit).

Unit 12

The first two exercises practise the contrast between the present simple tense for habitual actions and the present continuous for a current action. Note that the change described in Exercises 1 and 2 is a temporary change only. The use of the present simple for the usual action indicates that it will continue after the disruption of the strike. Exercise 4(ii) uses the contrast again.

Exercises 3 and 4 practise comparatives in the context of making recommendations. Exercise 5 is fairly open. Some students (eg those following this course in England) might use the structures of Exercise 1: 'I usually eat .... but during my stay in England I am eating ....'. However, a general essay could incorporate some of the material from earlier units, eg strings of adjectives, classifying different kinds of food, using generalisations and examples, etc.

Further work Students might like to describe their own experiences in changing habits, eg giving up smoking. If they wish to describe a permanent change of habit, they have to use the past simple or *used to* for the former habit: 'I smoked (or: used to smoke) forty cigarettes a day, but now I chew chewing gum instead.'

Unit 13

Preliminary work for this unit could consider two or more newspapers in the students' own language, where possible, and contrast how they present the same news item differently. Points to note are: (a) what facts are included, (b) what prominence is given to one or two facts, (c) whether the facts are presented in a logical (eg chronological) order or re-arranged for emphasis, (d) the language of the headlines. In Exercises 1 and 2 there is no ideal order. Each variation simply gives a different effect. For instance, in Exercise 2, two of the newspapers emphasise the fact that the inventors were children and that they won a prize, while the third emphasises the scientific nature of their claim. The third is from a more 'highbrow' newspaper than the other two. The most efficient way of approaching Exercise 2(i) is to take each headline in turn, and, selecting one newspaper first, make notes of the main facts relevant to headline. Then, move to the second newspaper, and, again taking each headline in turn, add to the notes any *additional* items that were not included in the first newspaper. Repeat this procedure with the third newspaper. Finally, use the notes to write a complete account. It will be up to the teacher to decide whether and to what extent students should use the actual wording of the newspapers. Exercise 3(ii) asks for a summary and it is assumed that students will use the headlines as a guide.

Further work For summarising it is useful to: (i) underline main points in the original, (ii) make a list of headings, (iii) compress information into fewer sentences. The last skill is the most difficult, since it often requires the use of complex sentence patterns. The best procedure is for the teacher to write a summary of a chosen passage in advance, observe what structures he himself used, and drill them before students do their own summarising.

Unit 14

Requesting and giving advice can use many different expressions and there is no simple way of deciding which is better in any context. Those that use personal pronouns, as in Exercise 1, are less formal than others like 'It is advisable to ....', or 'It is important to/that ....', or 'It is recommended that people ....' The expressions listed in the unit are among the more common.

Further work Exercises 2 and 3 deal with a very simple paragraph plan. Each part of that plan could be expanded into an independent paragraph and an essay could be developed out of the short paragraphs in Exercises 1, 2, and 3.

Unit 15

The early exercises in this unit rely on an intelligent selection of relevant information, in this case put into very short paragraphs. Students should note that a paragraph may consist of just one sentence. Of the three letters in Exercise 2, the first is the best since it gives relevant information clearly, uses correct style ('Madam', 'Yours faithfully') and gives the full name of the writer at the end. The second gives less information and uses the matron's name with 'Yours sincerely' at the end. This is not usual unless there has been some previous contact with her. The last letter does not say what the writer really wants. 'Dear Matron' is only used by nurses and doctors working in the same hospital. 'Yours' and the first name at the end of a letter is restricted to personal letters.

Exercise 3 shows some genuine English advertisements. 'LVs' in the SECRETARY advertisement are 'Luncheon Vouchers' — tickets that are accepted by some restaurants in payment for meals. Employers give them to staff as a tax-free benefit. The advertisement for 'Waitresses m/f' shows an amusing confusion cause by the English law under which it is illegal for an employer to discriminate against either sex. The abbreviation 'm/f' means 'male or female', yet 'waitresses' is feminine!

Further work Students usually enjoy role-play, so Exercises 4 and 5 could be extended to interviews for other jobs, or for selection as a member of a sports club, or for selection as a candidate to represent a town in an election, or for receipt of social benefits such as free housing, free university education, etc.

Unit 16

The paragraph to be written in Exercise 1(ii) practises generalisations followed by supporting examples, one of the most common patterns in written English. After Exercises 2 and 3 have introduced some necessary sentence constructions, that pattern is extended in Exercises 4 and 5 to the plan of a whole essay, where the first paragraph describes the generalisation and the following paragraphs support it.

Further work It is useful for students to do some analysis of given essays, letters or other writing. They should look for the generalisations and the supporting examples, which may, of course, not occur in the order used in this unit. They should then make a plan similar to the one illustration in Exercise 4. Then they put aside the original essay and try to reproduce it from the plan.

Unit 17

Writing instructions is very similar to describing a process, except that imperative verb forms are frequently used as in Exercises 1 and 2. Exercises 3 and 4 demonstrate a sentence construction that allows information to be compressed instead of separated in short simple sentences. Students should try to use this construction in Exercise 5.

Further work Not all instructions use the imperative. For instance, the passive is also common, eg 'The washing is put into the machine and the door is shut tight.' Students could rewrite the instructions in the unit in the passive voice.

Unit 18

Units 18, 19, and 20 are the most challenging in this book and should act as a bridge to *Writing in English 3*. Unit 18 suggests a number of techniques for starting, developing and ending an essay. There are more suggestions in *Teaching English Writing* especially in Chapter 3, Section 3.2. The development section of the essay in this unit requires classification of people's fears and of examples from the history of mechanisation. The Fear of Machines chart does not show any classification, but students can observe that two examples deal with laws, three with attacks related to inventions, and three with people's expressed opinions. The Mechanisation Chart shows classifications according to the headings of the sections and columns.

Further work Other topics should be found to practise whatever openings and closings the students did not use in the work of this unit.

Unit 19

This unit relates writing to speaking. Although there are very important differences between speech and written English, the context of a debate normally requires rather formal language and it is therefore acceptable to read the speeches. However, the major contrasts with essay-style or narrative should be preserved: (1) direct address to the listeners using 'you', and (2) contractions — even if full forms are actually written down, speakers should use contractions when reading aloud.

The unit builds up the speeches gradually, from a preliminary listing of ideas, to exemplifications, and writing the introduction after the main speech. Students should follow the steps in the order given.

If students have never taken part in a debate before, they should, if possible, hold one in the native language first.

Further work A similar approach can be used for other topics of interest to the class.

Unit 20

The writing in this unit is only very slightly guided. Real tourist brochures should be looked at if possible and the techniques noted. The exercises gradually build up the material needed for a brochure and should be done in the order suggested.

Further work A real brochure could be used as a model and adapted for another town, eg a brochure about London could be re-worked to suit the students' own city. Other work could include a leaflet about the school for visitors coming to a centenary celebration, or about the local museum, or art gallery, town hall, etc.

Unit 1

Narrative: describing people and events
Linking sentences using *first*, *next*, *then*, *after that*, *finally*

Henry VIII (Henry the Eighth) was King of England from 1509 till his death in 1549. He was a very big, fat man, but he was very intelligent and educated and a most powerful king. For example, he was able to put most of his enemies — and two of his wives — into the Tower of London. They usually stayed there until their heads were cut off.

Henry wanted his family to rule England after his death so he needed a son. That was one of the reasons for his many wives.

Henry VIII

Marriages *First*, in 1509, Henry married Catherine of Aragon. She was a very religious woman, but she gave him only a daughter, and no son. So Henry divorced her. *Next*, he married Ann Boleyn in 1533. She was a very pretty brunette. However, she didn't have any sons either. So Henry found a reason to put her in the Tower. They cut off her head in 1536. *Then*, in 1536, Henry married Jane Seymour, a kind, quiet woman. She finally gave Henry a son and he later became Edward VI. Unfortunately Jane Seymour herself died in 1537.

Catherine of Aragon

Ann Boleyn

Jane Seymour

Exercise 1
Completion

Now copy out the story of Henry VIII and his wives and then write the second half of the story yourself. Use these pictures below. The main words for each sentence are in brackets. Choose the correct form of the verbs and add your own words where necessary.

After that .... 1539 Henry .... (marry) Anne of Cleves. She .... (be) young, but she .... (be) not very .... Henry .... (be) not happy. So he .... (divorce) her .... 1540. *Then* he .... (marry) Catherine Howard. She .... (be) 21 years old with .... eyes, and .... hair. However, there were bad rumours about her behaviour, so Henry .... (send) her .... the Tower. They .... (cut off) her head .... 1542. *Finally*, Henry .... (marry) Catherine Parr .... 1542. She had .... hair and was .... She was his sixth wife and he was her .... (three) husband. When Henry died in 1549, she .... (be) still his wife.

Anne of Cleves

Catherine Howard

Catherine Parr

Exercise 2
Completion

Note: The history of Henry VIII's wives in Exercise 1 was in *six* parts. Each part was about one wife and started with one of the words: *first*, *next*, *then*, *after that*, *finally*. These are called LINKING WORDS.

The six parts followed each other in the right order according to the dates, and each part said something about one wife and her marriage to Henry.

Similarly, each of the six pictures on the left shows something that spoiled Susan's morning. Write the story. Fill in the blanks, putting the verbs in their correct form and adding any necessary words. Use *each* of the LINKING WORDS. Pay attention to the punctuation.

Susan's Unlucky Morning

...., Susan's alarm clock .... (not wake) her. It was an old .... and the .... was broken. So Susan had to hurry. ...., Susan .... (spill) the coffee while she .... (have) breakfast. It .... (ruin) her dress, and Susan had to change her clothes. ...., the car .... (not start) because it was cold outside. Susan had to ask a neighbour to help her. ...., Susan .... (drive) quickly because she was late. But there was a traffic jam, which .... (waste) twenty minutes. So she .... (run) into her office building. ...., she .... (see) that the lift was out of order, and she had to walk up five floors. ...., she .... (arrive) in her office, half an hour late. She was very tired. But it did not matter. It was a holiday. She .... (not remember) this until she .... (reach) the office!

Exercise 3
Guided writing

The next pictures are not in the correct order. Decide which ought to be the first and last pictures. The others can go in any order you choose.
Write the story of *The Polite Thieves* using *each* of the LINKING WORDS.

Exercise 4
Writing game

First,
Next,
Then,
After that,
Then,
Finally,

Fold a sheet of paper into six parts and write one of the LINKING WORDS at the beginning of each part. Now choose a title for a story. Then let six students in turn write one or two sentences in each part. Each student should fold the paper when he has finished so that the next student sees only his own part. Read the whole story. This is fun when everybody writes strange or unusual things. It is an English party game called 'Consequences'.

Unit 2

Descriptions with contrasts
Reference words: *it, they, one/ones*

Steve is helping his Swedish friends who want to come and study in London.

104 Abbey Road,
London SW7.
18th August, 1983

Dear Gunnar and Ingrid,

I'm trying very hard to find you a flat in London for your year's study here. It's difficult, but don't worry. I think I've found something.

Yesterday I went to see two flats in Hammersmith. I think they are suitable because they are both near the hospital where you will study, but the first one is not in a good position. It's on a quiet street, but it's a long way from the underground station and from the nearest children's school. However, the flat itself is large and modern. It has big rooms, with nice furniture.

The second one is on a very busy street. It's near the underground station and the school, but the building itself is old. The flat has medium-sized rooms, and only basic furniture. On the other hand, its much cheaper than the first one: only £80 per week instead of £110.

I asked the estate agent to wait for my answer, so please write quickly. Tell me which flat you prefer.

Hoping to hear from you soon,

Yours, Steve

Exercise 1 Completion

(i) This is a plan of Steve's letter. Use Steve's letter opposite to complete it.

Underlining

(ii) Some important words in the plan are underlined. Find them in Steve's letter and underline them there too.

The Flats	Good points		Bad points
both			
place	They are suitable because .... both		
the first one			
place	It's ....,	but	it's .... and
features	However .... and ..... It .... with		
the second one			
place	It's near		is on ....
features			but the building ..... The flat has .... and ....
cost	On the other hand ... . the first one:		

Exercise 2 Sentence matching

(i) When Steve contrasts the flats he uses the words: *but*, *However*, *On the other hand*. You will see these words in the second column below. Link one part from the first column with one part from the second column. Check your answers in Steve's letter.

a It's near the Underground Station and a school,
b It's on a quiet street,
c It's on a quiet street, far from the Underground and the school.
d It has two average-sized rooms and only basic furniture.
e They're both near Hammersmith,

1 On the other hand, it's much cheaper than the first flat.
2 but the first one is not central.
3 However, the flat itself is large and in good condition.
4 but the building itself is old.
5 but it's far from the Underground station and from the school.

(ii) Write some sentences using *but*. Link any part from the first column with any part from the second column.

a Her blue dress has a beautiful pattern
b The sofa in the flat is modern
c Clive's notebook has a bright red cover

but

1 it's torn in several places.
2 it's not very clean.
3 it looks old and worn.

(iii) Match the sentences from the two columns and link them by starting the second one with either *However* or *On the other hand*.

a She always helps her friends in trouble.
b Judy would like to visit her cousin in Oslo.
c We might climb some of the big mountains in Europe this summer.

However, On the other hand,

1 if there's not enough time, we might just tour the capital cities.
2 it's an expensive trip, so she may have to meet her in Holland.
3 she never asks anyone else for help.

Exercise 3
Sentence arrangement

Use the following to write a paragraph. You will have to change the order and add punctuation.

The flat is much larger than the one we have now
We're moving into a new flat next week
but just as noisy
but not into a quieter district
because it's on the first floor
because I'll still be able to see all my good friends
However, I'm glad we're staying in the same district

Exercise 4
Guided writing

Your cousins want to come for a month's visit to your city. They will bring their two children too. They can stay at your house or at your uncle's. They want to know which house is closer to the centre of the city and to an underground station or bus stop, and which has more space for them all.

(i) Imagine the two houses, and then fill in the information in this outline.

Your house
1 .... centre ....
2 .... station ....
3 .... However,/On the other hand ....

Your uncle's house
1 .... centre ....
2 .... station ....
3 .... However,/On the other hand ....

(ii) *Now write a letter to your cousin* explaining about the two houses. Follow this plan (which also fits the letter from Steve at the start of the unit).

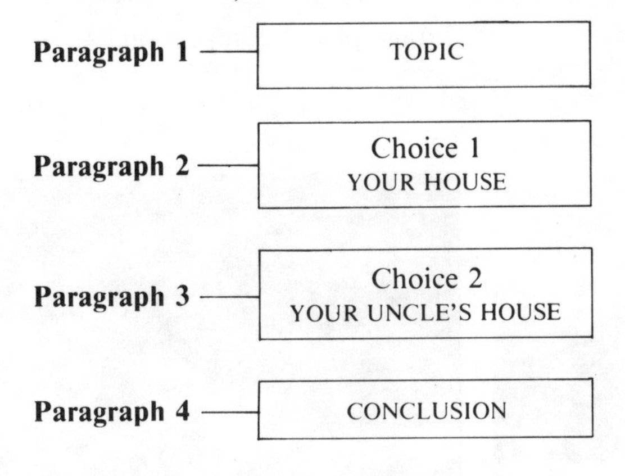

Exercise 5
Describing a picture

Look at this picture of a robot.

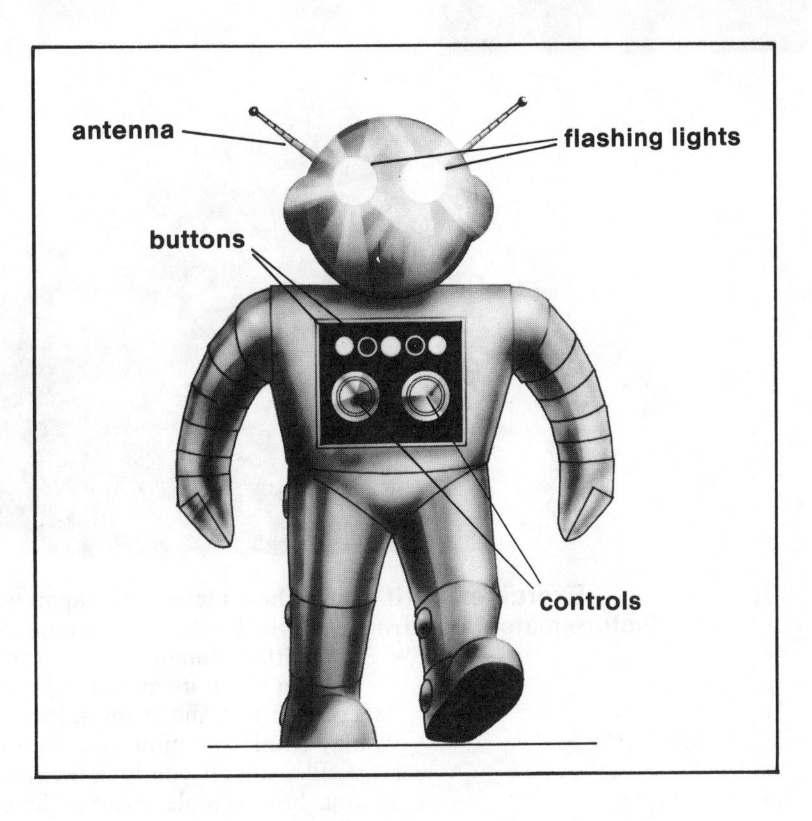

(i) Draw a picture of another robot. Make some parts the same and some different from the robot in the picture, eg give your robot more arms, or eyes, or put the eyes in a different place, etc.
Do not let anyone see your picture!

(ii) Write a description of your picture, explaining which parts are the same as and which are different from the robot on this page. Use some or all of these words: *both robots, the first robot, the second robot, and, but, however, on the other hand.*

Exercise 6
Writing game

Give your description to another student and take his/her description.
Each of you should now try to draw the other's robot, using the information in the description. When you have finished, show each other the drawings and correct them if necessary. (If your description was not clear enough, try to improve it.)

Unit 3

Describing a place
Generalisations and examples
Paragraphs of comparison

1

2

3

Exercise 1
Picture matching

(i) Match these pictures of Japan with the following descriptions from a tourist book, by matching the numbers with the letters.

A In addition, Japan is also a sportsman's paradise. For example, you can ski in its mountains and skate on its lakes in winter. You can fish and swim in its rivers in summer, and you can play tennis and hunt in the autumn.

B Besides this, if you love the theatre, Japan is just the place for you. For example, there is the very old Noh theatre, where the actors wear masks on stage. In addition, you can see the Kabuki theatre where men play all the women's parts.

C Japan is a wonderful country. For example, nature lovers will find high mountains, more than 1000 lakes and rivers, and many hot springs and there are 17 large national parks.

(ii) Write out the three paragraphs, following the order of the pictures.

(iii) Underline every use of the LINKING WORDS *for example*, *in addition*, *besides this*, and check these meanings in each paragraph.

Meanings

1 'For example' is used after a general statement, before examples which illustrate it.
2 'In addition' means 'also'. It usually joins things which are *similar* and could belong in one list.
3 'Besides this' is almost the same as 'in addition', but it frequently joins *different* things.

Exercise 2
Sentence linking

Link each sentence from the first column with a suitable sentence from the second column. Use the linking words from Exercise 1.

1	One of the main attractions of Scotland is its wild landscape.	**a**	The buildings of the city are themselves like a great museum of architecture.
2	The museums of Paris have some of the most famous art in the world.	**b**	You can easily reach any other country on the Mediterranean from the port of Piraeus.
3	London today is one of the 'eating capitals' of the world.	**c**	You can travel through miles of mountains, rushing water, and jungle-like vegetation.
4	In Greece you can see wild mountains, ruins of ancient cities, and the life of modern Athens	**d**	You can have Indian curry, Chinese duck, Japanese sukiyaki, Greek dolmades, and hundreds of other foods.

Exercise 3
Linking words

Read this description of Tokyo, the capital of Japan, and put a circle around the best linking words.

Tokyo, the world's biggest city in population, is a city of contrasts. *Besides this/For example*, you can visit the very beautiful temples and gardens that are hundreds of years old. *On the other hand/For example*, in the same city you can buy anything you want on the Ginza, Tokyo's mile-long street of modern shops. *Besides this/For example*, Tokyo's night life gives you exciting entertainment of all kinds.

Exercise 4
Guided writing

Write these sentences about Holland in the correct order, making one paragraph.

On the other hand, the countryside is full of old windmills, medieval castles, and villages where people still wear the old Dutch costumes.
Holland is an interesting mixture of the new and the old.
For example, you can enjoy the cities' modern shops, and exciting nightclubs, cabarets and discotheques.
In addition, you can sail around Holland along the dykes in the oldest form of transport.

Exercise 5
Free writing

Write a paragraph about your country, or your city, or another city that you know, similar to the paragraph in either Exercise 3 or Exercise 4.

Unit 4

Narrative
Comparing people

Exercise 1
Personality quiz

Most people want to learn about themselves. Often there are questionnaires in magazines, like this. Answer these questions for yourself.

Personality Corner
Rate yourself. How much do you talk?

1 If you hear a secret, do you tell somebody?
   a often **b** sometimes **c** never
2 With your friends, do you talk more than anyone else?
   a often **b** usually **c** not usually
3 Do you friends ever say, 'Excuse me, can I say something?'
   a often **b** never **c** sometimes

Now check your answers. Here is the table for scores. The numbers in the boxes are the scores.

	Question 1	Question 2	Question 3
a	3	3	3
b	2	2	1
c	1	1	2

YOUR TOTAL . . . .

Your Personality
TOTAL 3: You are a quiet person. Talk more!
TOTAL 4–6: You are a good listener. You talk, but you also listen.
TOTAL 7–9: You talk too much! You are a chatterbox. Perhaps you are an unpopular chatterbox.

A How do you choose friends?
Place a tick (√) in the box next to the choice you prefer.

Do you prefer
a) people who share your attitudes and beliefs? ☐
OR
b) people who have attitudes and beliefs which are different from your own? ☐

Do you prefer
a) people who have the same hobbies and interests as yourself? ☐
OR
b) people who have different hobbies and interests? ☐

Do you prefer
a) people who are your intellectual equals? ☐
b) people more intellectual than yourself? ☐
c) people less intellectual than yourself? ☐

Do you prefer
a) people who are religious? ☐
OR
b) people who do not have a religion? ☐

Do you prefer
a) people who enjoy taking risks? ☐
OR
b) people who avoid risks? ☐

Do you prefer
a) a small group of close friends? ☐
OR
b) a wide circle of acquaintances? ☐

B How do you see yourself?
Place a tick in the box to show how you see yourself.

	Most of the time	Sometimes	Never
1 honest			
2 generous			
3 patient			
4 ambitious			
5 friendly			
6 anxious			
7 sensitive			
8 lonely			
9 moody			
10 shy			
11 secretive			
12 unlucky			
13 stubborn			
14 open-minded			

Exercise 2
Personality quiz

Choose a partner, and ask him/her each question in **A** and put a tick in the box next to the answer.
Then ask questions for each point in **B**.
eg Are you a generous / (an) honest } person most of the time, sometimes, or never?
Put ticks in the boxes to show the answer.

Exercise 3
Guided writing

Now write a description of your partner, using his/her answers to Exercises 1 and 2. It is not necessary to include *all* the answers to the questions, only the most important information. This is an example of a description.

Andrew *is a* very flexible *person, because* he *prefers* people who have attitudes and beliefs which are different from his own. *In addition*, he *prefers* people with different hobbies and interests. *Besides this*, he *is a* friendly young man, *who likes to have* a wide circle of acquaintances. *However*, he only likes people who are intellectual, and he is a good listener. He is honest, *because*, for example, he admits that he is impatient and careless.

You may need these opposites:

honest	dishonest	generous	mean
patient	impatient	ambitious	unambitious
friendly	unfriendly	anxious	carefree
sensitive	thick-skinned	lonely	(no opposite)
moody	even-tempered	shy	confident
secretive	open	careless	careful
lucky	unlucky	stubborn	flexible

Exercise 4
Free writing

Exchange your description with one student after another until you find one that is very different from yours and of the opposite sex if possible. Work together with that student and write a comparison of the two people in your two descriptions. Use expressions like: *but, however, on the other hand, for example, in addition.*
Note: The two people may have one or two characteristics which are similar. You can use expressions like:

Ian and George are both . . .
Both Ian and George are . . . .
In one way, however, Ian and George are similar, because they both . . . .

Exercise 5
Free writing

Now, if your two people were of the opposite sex, imagine that they are strangers and that they met on a 'blind date' (a meeting between strangers, arranged by a friend who thinks that they might like each other). Write a story about what happened. Start like this:

When . . . . and . . . . met on a blind date, they began to argue at once. *First*, ... said 'I prefer . . . .', but . . . . replied 'I'm sorry, I prefer . . . .'. *Next*, ...

Continue the story, using *then, after that, finally*.

If your two people were not of the opposite sex, imagine that one visited the other and they argued about where to go out. Start your story:

When . . . . visited . . . ., they argued at once about where to go in the evening. *First*, ...

and carry on in the same way as the other story.

Unit 5

Narrative
Time sequence signals: *while, in the meantime, all of a sudden, in the end*

2 Bedford Road,
London NW1.
23rd June, 1983

Dear Gregori,

I must tell you about a car accident I saw yesterday right in the centre of London. Oh, don't worry! No one was hurt. In fact, it wasn't serious at all. It just seemed so British, I think. At least, it could never happen like that at home!

This is the beginning of a letter from Helena, an overseas student in London, to her boyfriend at home.

Exercise 1
Picture matching

Now help Helena to finish her letter. First, fill in the correct forms of the verbs in the sentences. Then, match the short paragraphs with the pictures. The pictures are in the correct order; the paragraphs are not.

Write out the whole letter and finish it correctly with *yours, love,* or *lots of love*, and *Helena* at the bottom.

a *Then*, of course, the two drivers (get) .... out. The middle-aged one (look) .... very upset, but not angry. They (begin) .... to check the damage to their cars, and to exchange information.

b It was about 10.30 in the morning. I was just standing near the lions in Trafalgar Square. I (mind) .... my own business, and (enjoy) .... the sun.

c *In the meantime* an enormous traffic jam (form) .... behind them. But, unbelievable as it may seem, no one (toot) .... his horn. The British are so calm!

d *All of a sudden* a car (stall) .... in the middle of the road.

e Then another car (come) .... round the corner and (crash) .... right into the first, *while* the driver (try) .... to start the car again.

f *In the end* the two drivers (shake) .... hands, (get) .... into their cars and (drive) .... away. The traffice jam slowly (clear) .... up.

Exercise 2
Underlining

(i) There are several linking words in Helena's letter.
then introduces an event that occurs *after* another event.
while introduces an event that occurs *at the same time as* another event.
in the meantime introduces an event that occurs *in the time between the start and end* of another event.
all of a sudden introduces an event that occurs *without warning.*
in the end introduces *the last of a number of* events.
Note: while links two parts of one sentence. The other linking words usually start a new sentence.
Find all these linking words in the letter and underline them.

Sentence joining

(ii) Use one of the linking words in 2(i) to connect these sentences (or parts of sentences), and write them out.

1	First Jeff opened the door very quietly	**a**	the father hurried to fetch a doctor
2	The mother cooked some soup for the sick child	**b**	the fire alarm rang
3	The doorbell rang	**c**	she was bathing the baby
4	I lost my wallet in the street and looked everywhere for it	**d**	I reported the loss to the police
5	We were having a history lesson	**e**	he tiptoed into the room
6	At 11 pm they met in the cellar to share out the stolen money	**f**	the door burst open and the police rushed in

Exercise 3
Guided writing

A plan for a story might be:

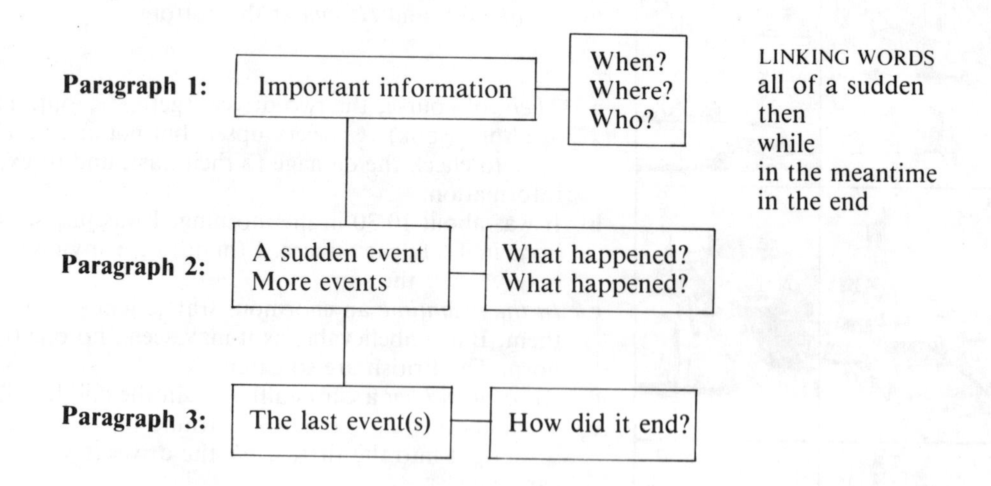

Here are sentences grouped together to make three paragraphs of a story. First, write numbers to show the correct order of the sentences in each paragraph.
Next decide the order of the paragraphs following the plan above.
Then write out the story.
Note: You have to join some sentences.

In the bus, some people were reading, one was eating, and a few were just looking out of the window.
During the Easter holiday, I took a bus tour to Wales.
No one talked to anyone else.

While he was making a phone call . . . .
In the end a new bus arrived and we had a wonderful time.
. . . . we started to talk to each other, and we became quite friendly.

. . . . there was a noise and the bus stopped.
Then the driver told us he had to telephone for a new bus.
All of a sudden, about ten kilometres outside London,
The driver got out to check.
In the meantime, the passengers were still reading or eating.

Exercise 4
Guided writing

Write a story about a party. Follow the plan in Exercise 3, and choose some of the information from these lists:

Paragraph 1

When? Saturday night — last week — Bank Holiday weekend
Where? At Mary and Linda's flat — in the north of London — at a hall which was hired by my boss
Who? People from the office with husbands and wives — my boss and his wife — some strange-looking people from different countries — a very tall dark man — a short bald man — a blonde beauty
What were they doing? dancing — drinking — talking — eating — flirting

Paragraph 2

A sudden event Two of the wives began to argue loudly — the short bald man began to sing — five uninvited guests came in — the next-door neighbour came to complain about the noise — the Swedish students started a non-stop dancing contest — two of the hostess' children came and started to dance in their pyjamas
More events
— the bald man's wife tried to pull him out of the room
— one spilled lemonade on the other
— the host asked them to leave, but they refused
— some of the other students joined in and cheered
— they went into the kitchen and started tasting everything
— the host explained and apologised, but it didn't help
— the noise was getting louder and louder
— dancing was getting faster
— everyone continued eating and drinking

Paragraph 3 *The last events*

— the neighbour joined the party
— the children fell asleep on the carpet
— the Swedes started folk-dancing
— the uninvited guests helped to clear up
— the husbands took their angry wives home
— the bald man fell asleep on the sofa
— everyone went home

Exercise 5
Free writing

Think of a story about:
A morning at a government office
or An aeroplane accident
or A football match
or any other events you like.
Try to write a plan first. Then write the story and use the linking words that were in the stories in this unit.

Unit 6

Factual reporting

Note-taking

Speech *versus* writing

Mrs O'Toole saw a bank robbery. She talked to Sergeant Foster at the Police Station and he taped her evidence. This is what was on the tape:

'Oh Officer! It was terrible! We get up in the morning, we plan our day, and we never expect danger? [1]I mean, at 11.30 in the morning! Oh, it was terrible.'

'What did you see, Mrs O'Toole?'

'What did I see? Oh, yes. [2]The robbery, of course, at the Bank. I work there. [3]I mean, at the corner near the Bank. My newspaper stand is there, right on the corner of Hill Road and Carlton Park Road. Oh, they were awful! [4]Those guns! [5]And those stocking masks! They were wearing stocking masks, all three of them. [6]Couldn't see their faces. But I did notice their hands. [7]Always notice hands. [8]You know, when people pay for my newspapers. Anyway, one of the robbers, the tall *thin* one —'

'How many were tall?'

'[9]Two. [10]One thin, one muscular. They were 1.80 m at least. Well, the thin one had long fine fingers like a piano-player. When they ran out of the Bank, this one stood next to me for a minute, holding his gun. [11]Long thin fingers.'

'Did you see the third one, Mrs O'Toole?'

'[12]The third one? [13]Didn't see him very well. He was shorter, I'm sure. They got into a van quickly.'

'Did you see the van? What colour was it?'

'[14]A light colour. [15]Beige perhaps, or off-white.'

'Thank you, Mrs O'Toole'.

Exercise 1
Note taking

(i) These are Sergeant Foster's notes:

Time
11 am
January

Place
The Bank
Corner Hill Rd and Carlton Park Rd

What witness said
Saw bank robbery by three armed masked men who escaped in van.

What witness was doing
Selling newspapers in newspaper stand next to bank

Description Two tall, one short robber, 1.80 m. at least, wearing beige stocking masks, one with long fingers.

Underline all these facts in Mrs O'Toole's evidence. Has Sergeant Foster made any mistakes? Has he added anything that Mrs O'Toole did not say? Is there anything unclear in the evidence? (How many guns did she see?) What kind of things did he omit?

Sentence completion

(ii) When we write, we normally use complete sentences. But when we speak we often shorten our sentences. The sentences in the dialogue that are numbered from 1 to 15 are all shortened. Use the following words or phrases to help you write out a complete sentence for each one. This will make the meaning of each sentence clear, but the complete forms would probably not occur in this kind of dialogue.

we never expect danger; I saw; I work; were awful; I; I always notice hands; were tall; was; he had; did I see; it was.

Exercise 2
Sentence completion

(i) Here is the report which Sergeant Foster wrote. Fill in the spaces with information from his notes. Where there are two linking words, choose one.

Metropolitan Police **File no.** 654

On 12 January 1983, Mrs O'Toole was on the corner of .... and ....

She says that at .... am, ... men .... out of the .... They were all wearing .... over their faces. In addition/However, Mrs O'Toole claims that one of the robbers had a .... First/Then they all got into a .... and drove away. The witness thinks that the van was .... or ...., but/for example she is not sure.

The witness remembers that one of the robbers was .... and .... and the other was tall and .... (about .... in height), and the third was .... Besides/In addition, she claims that the second one had ....

Officer-in-charge... M. Foster.......

(ii) Why is Sergeant Foster's report shorter than Mrs O'Toole's taped evidence?

Exercise 3
Reported speech

In Sergeant Foster's report, there are four *verbs of saying*:

She *says* Mrs O'Toole *claims* The witness *thinks*
remembers

They are all in the *present tense* because they mean:

Mrs O'Toole *believes* this.
She will say the same thing again if you ask her.

But the verbs in the rest of the report are in the *past tense* because the events were in the past.

Put the first verb in each of these sentences in the present tense and the second verb in the past tense:

1 Mr Brown (say) .... that he (see) .... the parcel in the corner.
2 They all (claim) .... that Joe (come) .... to the party at 9 pm.
3 The children (think) .... that the delivery man (ring) .... the doorbell before lunchtime.
4 Mary (remember) .... that Mrs Brody (be) .... in her shop at the time of the murder.

Exercise 4
Underlining

(i) The cashier of the Bank also gave evidence to Sergeant Foster. Read it and underline information about Time, Place, What Witness was Doing, What Witness Saw, and Description of Robbers (see Exercise 1).

'It was awful! [1]And so fast!'

'What can you remember?'

'[2]Well, when it began. I was checking what the time was. [3]10.55. I looked at the clock on the wall. Suddenly I noticed a man under the clock. He had a gun. [4]A very odd face, I thought. After a second, I realised that he was wearing a stocking mask over his face. He said very loudly, "Put your hands up and move over to the wall." That voice was interesting. [5]Deep and smooth. The other one — the short one — went to the cash desk and put all the money into two leather bags.'

'How short was he?'

'[6]About 1.30 m, I think. I'm not sure. But the other two were tall. This one — the short one — was strange. [7]Terribly nervous. [8]Didn't keep still.'

'What about the third one?'

'I can't remember the third one. [9]Hardly saw him. He was behind me. I know he was tall. He seemed bigger than the first one, the one with the gun. That one was thin.

Then they moved out of the Bank, backwards. That's about all I can tell you.'

Sentence completion

(ii) Find all shortened sentences (they are numbered 1 to 9) and write out each one in complete form. The sentence *before* each shortened sentence will help you to decide what word or phrase should be used.

Note: We can say: He was 1.80 m *tall*. but we cannot use *short* instead of *tall*, even when we mean that the person is short. We say:

He was 1.30 m.

Note-taking

(iii) Then, write out notes for Sergeant Foster's second report, as in Exercise 1. Write only the important words. Do not write complete sentences in the notes.
Include *only the facts* which the Sergeant needs.

Exercise 5
Guided writing

(i) Look at this paragraph from Sergeant Foster's report of the cashier's evidence. Do you think that it is the first paragraph? What are your reasons?

> The cashier says that after this, the short robber went to the cash desk and put all the money into two leather bags. The cashier remembers that he seemed terribly nervous because he didn't keep still.

Now use this paragraph and the notes you made, and write all of Sergeant Foster's report. Use the verbs *say, think, claim*, and *remember*, and some of the linking words: *in addition, besides, however, then, first, suddenly, while, but, in the end.*

Free writing

(ii) A few days later, a third witness suddenly came to see Sergeant Foster. He was *not near the Bank* on the day of the robbery. But he gave some very important information to Sergeant Foster.

Divide the class into groups of four or five. Each group should decide who the 'surprise witness' was. Then they should make notes about the information he gave to Sergeant Foster.

Finally, every group should write Sergeant Foster's report.

Unit 7

Using tabulations and comparing alternatives

Expressing possibilities

Exercise 1
Comprehension

Steve and June want to go to Paris for a few days before Easter. They wrote to the See-It-Now Travel Agency in London, and asked about some possible ways of going cheaply. This is part of the answer they got:

. . . . In answer to your enquiries about cheap fares from London to Paris, here are two possible methods of travel:

1 You can go by a combination of coach, ferry, and train. The ferry crosses the Channel from Dover to Calais, where you can get a train to Paris. The trip one way, from London to Paris, takes a bit more than ten hours, and a ticket costs £40.00. However, if you choose this way of travelling, you'll have to travel either on Friday or on Sunday.

2 Alternatively, you may want to go all the way by coach. The coach leaves from Victoria Station to Paris, takes fourteen hours, and a ticket costs £25.00. If you choose a coach trip, you'll be able to travel either on Thursday, Friday or Sunday.

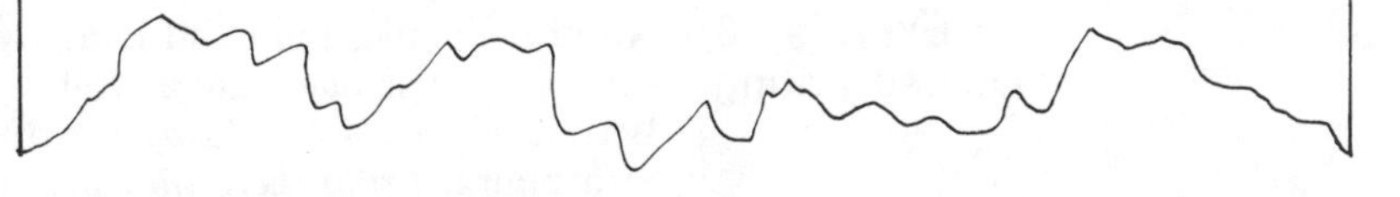

Fill in the following table with the information and the two suggestions given by the Travel Agency.

LONDON — PARIS

	A	B
	Coach, ferry, train	Through coach
Travel time		
Days of week		
Single fare		

Notice the words we can use for:

a	suggesting possibilities:	you *can* go you *may* want to go
b	showing alternatives:	*alternatively,* *either .... or*
c	showing results of a choice:	*If you choose .... you'll* (you will) have to

Exercise 2
Completion

A few days later, the travel agent found a third method of travel, and wrote to Steve and June again. Use the information in the table below to complete his letter.

See-It-Now

15 Wigmore Street
London W C 2

18 May 1983

Dear Mr and Mrs Bragg

I wonder if you have made any decisions about your trip to Paris. I sent you details of two methods of travel which would both be very pleasant.

Table:

	London — Paris
	Coach, Hovercraft and Train
Travel time	8 hours
Days of week	any
Single fare	£35

Exercise 3
Guided writing

Another couple, Paul and Eva, *are also going to Europe in the summer*. Their plans are as follows: *On 3 July, they* fly *to* West Berlin, *where they will stay for* three days *before flying to* Strasbourg. *From there they take a* boat *to* Paris, *arriving in* Paris *on* 9 July. *After* one *day in* Paris, *they take a* train *to* Lyons *and the next day continue by* train *to* Florence, *where they will stay* from 11 July to 13 July. *Their last stop is* Rome, *where they will spend* two days, 14 July to 16 July, *before flying home to* Copenhagen.

Use the information in Steve and June's itinerary below to write a paragraph similar to the one about Paul and Eva. Use as many of the italicised words as possible.

Itinerary

8 July	travel to Paris
12 July	plane to Venice
13 July	train to Florence
15 July	train to Milan
18 July	fly to London

Exercise 4
Guided writing

The two couples are friends and wish to meet in Europe. This is the first part of Paul and Eva's letter to Steve and June, suggesting some possible meeting-places.

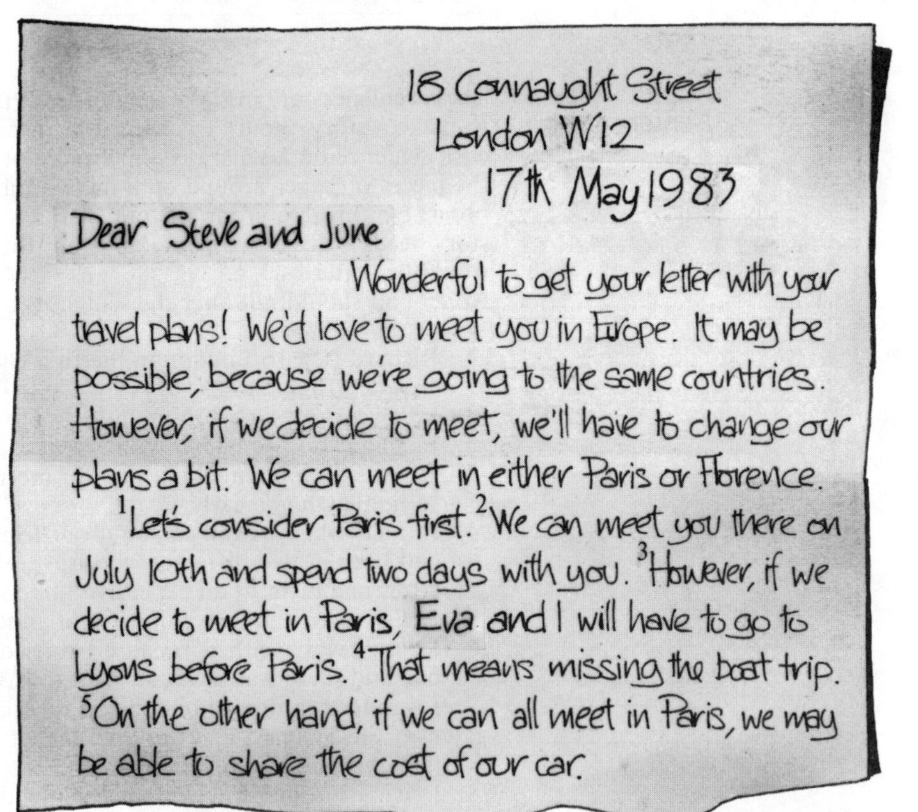

18 Connaught Street
London W12
17th May 1983

Dear Steve and June

Paragraph 1

Wonderful to get your letter with your travel plans! We'd love to meet you in Europe. It may be possible, because we're going to the same countries. However, if we decide to meet, we'll have to change our plans a bit. We can meet in either Paris or Florence.

Paragraph 2
1 Topic
2 Suggestion: time of meeting
3 Result of suggestion
4 Result of 3
5 Benefit of suggestion

[1] Let's consider Paris first. [2] We can meet you there on July 10th and spend two days with you. [3] However, if we decide to meet in Paris, Eva and I will have to go to Lyons before Paris. [4] That means missing the boat trip. [5] On the other hand, if we can all meet in Paris, we may be able to share the cost of our car.

Use the information in Exercise 3 to write a third paragraph for the letter, starting with '*Alternatively*', and suggesting a meeting in Florence. Follow the outline showing the structure of Paragraph 2. State the TOPIC, suggest a two-day meeting in Florence, and then describe the change of plans that June and Steve will have to make. Include a 'benefit of suggestion' that is different from the one in Paragraph 2.

Exercise 5
Writing activity

Students divide into pairs and ask each other:

(i) where they want to travel to

(ii) how much time they can spend

(iii) how much money they can spend.

Then they get information about methods of travel from a travel agency. (If this is not possible, they can invent the details.) Each student plans an itinerary for the other, and writes it in a paragraph similar to the one in Exercise 3.
When everyone is finished, students try to find another person in the class who wants to travel to the same place (or to a place fairly near) and then write to that person suggesting a meeting during the trip. (If no other student has chosen a suitable place, they should invent another person who has.)

Unit 8

Comparing two narratives

Comparing different composition plans

Exercise 1
Sentence order

These sentences are in the wrong order. Put them in the right order to make a story about 'Two trips to England.' If possible, write each sentence on a separate, small piece of paper, and then move the pieces of paper around on a table until you have the right order. Do this in a group of four or five students if you can. The story needs at least two paragraphs but three or four paragraphs would be better.
Note: You should *not* alter the sentences or add anything to them.

1 Richard flew to London in the first class; I was in a cheap, crowded flight.
2 Last year, my rich cousin and I both travelled separately to England, but we had very different experiences.
3 He was disappointed and tired of meeting only other tourists, so he flew home early.
4 In fact, when we talked about our trips later, we felt that we had been in two different worlds!
5 After one night at an expensive London hotel, he got a new Rolls-Royce and drove up to Scotland.
6 I didn't worry either, because I carried my old brown camping bag and there was always a field to sleep in.
7 I wandered around London for a week, living in a small hotel near the Thames, and explored the city by bus, by underground and on foot.
8 Driving through England and Scotland, Richard never had to worry about accommodation, because his travel agent had booked excellent hotels.
9 He found that he was paying high prices for meals; but twice a publican looked at my dirty shoes and untidy beard and then gave me a free drink.
10 What Richard did worry about was good food; so he only went to the big cities and the best restaurants.
11 Richard found the English people cold and unfriendly; I found them warm and generous.
12 But I will come back as soon as I can save more money.
13 I tried out the small pubs in little villages where the local people go.
14 He says he will never return to England.
15 I'm sure there are a thousand more villages to see.

Exercise 2
Composition planning

Look at these two plans. Does your arrangement of the sentences in Exercise 1 follow one of them? If not, draw the plan that you followed.

Plan 1

Paragraph 1	TOPIC SENTENCES	— cousins — trips to England — different experience — return?
Paragraph 2	DEVELOPMENT	— method of travel Richard . . . . 'I' — in London Richard . . . . 'I' — out of London Richard . . . . 'I' — accommodation Richard . . . . 'I' — food Richard . . . . 'I'
Paragraph 3	CONCLUSION	The English people Richard . . . . 'I' — home early (Richard)

Plan 2

Paragraph 1	TOPIC SENTENCES	— cousins — trips to England — different experiences — the English people — home early (Richard)
Paragraph 2	DEVELOPMENT	*The same as plan 1.*
Paragraph 3	CONCLUSION	— return? Richard . . . . 'I'

Exercise 3
Planned free writing

Write a letter from Richard to his mother, describing the differences between his own trip and his poorer cousin's trip. Follow one of the plans in Exercise 2, or your own plan if you drew a different one.

Exercise 4
Planned free writing

This is the beginning of a story:

> Cartland's hands were on my shoulders, holding me and pulling me back from the darkness.
> 'You're alive', he murmured. 'Thank God.'
> My tongue tasted like clay. It was dry and immovable in the cave of my mouth, and all the hammers in the world were at work just behind my eyes.
> 'Wait', Cartland said, 'Hold still, turn your head this way. That's better. Now.'

Prepare to complete the story.

(i) First, make your mind up about these points:

1 The story could tell what happened just before Cartland helped the story-teller, or it could tell what happens next (with only a very quick explanation about what happened before). Which do you prefer?
2 Was the darkness real, or was the story-teller unconscious?
3 Is Cartland a good friend, or is he really an enemy?
4 Why is the story-teller's tongue dry? Why does his head hurt?
5 Why does Cartland say, 'Turn your head this way'? Does he want the story-teller to look at something? Does he want to pull him out of a hole in the ground? Does he want to give him a drink? Does he want to put a bandage on his head?

(ii) Now make a plan for your story.

Exercise 5

Write the story.

Unit 9

Classifying

Giving advice

On 27 March 1980, there was a terrible accident to an oil rig, the 'Alexander Kielland' in the North Sea.

These are the radio signals from the rig and from a rescue helicopter.

From the Alexander Kielland:

5.50 pm — 'This is the Alexander Kielland. We are in trouble. Calling all ships. S.O.S.'

6.20 pm — 'This is the Alexander Keilland. We are sinking. Calling all ships. S.O.S. Wind 40 km. Waves 7 m.'

A rescue helicopter on radio to base:

7.15 pm — 'Fifteen ships now helping the Alexander Keilland. Several helicopters and more ships moving towards the area. We will save them.'

11 pm — 'Parts of the rig breaking up in the sea. Several bodies in the water. Great danger to the ships. Very dark.'

11.51 pm — 'One leg of the Alexander Keilland floating in the water. The Alexander Keilland under the water.'

7.50 am — '103 people saved. 7 dead, 115 still missing.'

Exercise 1
Completion

Michael Stevens is a young engineer. He wants to work on an oil rig in the North Sea. His father is worried about the danger. Use the information from the previous passage to help you complete the conversation between the father and son:

Mr Stevens What did the Director tell you about the oil rig?
Michael He said it .... quite safe.
Mr Stevens Really! I thought oil rigs .... safe until the accident in 1980.
Michael At that time the rigs were not prepared for accidents. Today things are different.
Mr Stevens Nonsense. The Alexander Kielland was very well prepared. Late in the afternoon, hours before the accident, they signalled that ....
Michael But only about half-an-hour later they signalled again, saying that .... and that .... They asked .... to help immediately.
Mr Stevens The ships arrived quickly. About one and a half hours after the first signal for help, a rescue helicopter reported that .... In addition, several .... and more .... towards the area. Everyone believed that they .... save all the people, even in such terrible conditions.
Michael They .... too late. By 11 pm, the helicopter crew observed that .... and noticed that .... They warned that .... because ....
Mr Stevens There was an army of rescuers.
Michael But they were not well prepared for accidents. They were .... late. Before midnight, they saw that .... and by the morning they .... only 103 out of 225 people.
Mr Stevens So what is better today?
Michael Everyone is more careful. The Director said that they .... very well prepared for accidents, but of course they don't expect any more accidents.
Mr Stevens There are many other jobs in the world! You don't need this one!

Exercise 2
Picture matching

This is a conversation between a doctor and a patient who has backache. Use the pictures opposite to complete it. All the words you need are in the box with the pictures.

Doctor There is nothing wrong with your back. Your .... is the problem.
Patient Well, I'm glad that there is nothing wrong with my back. How can I .... my posture?
Doctor Look at this chart. There are four main types of posture to consider: .... ing, ... ing, ... ing near or at .... level, and .... ing down. You have been .... ing your back muscles. You have to learn to keep your back muscles ....
Patient I will try to remember.
Doctor Even when resting, I mean .... ing or .... ing down, try .... keep your .... straight. You can .... your back by .... ing *in* the chair, not .... ing forward and .... ing your back. And get a hard bed. It will help by .... ing your body straight.

Patient I will put a board under my mattress.
Doctor And get a small pillow.
Patient Actually, I do use a small pillow already.
Doctor Fine. And don't forget your back when .... ing. If you .... working near ground ...., bend your knees, and if you are .... ing at .... level, ... like a baby.
Patient I can see that I have to change all my bad habits.
Doctor You will avoid a lot of pain.

Correcting you posture Keep your back straight! Help your back! Don't strain your muscles!	
WRONG RIGHT	When lifting things off the ground: — *Don't* bend the back — *Do* bend the knees and keep the back straight
WRONG RIGHT	When sitting: — *Don't* slide forward and curve your back — *Do* sit *in* the chair with your back straight
WRONG RIGHT	When working near ground level: — *Don't* bend the back — *Do* bend the knees and keep the back straight
WRONG RIGHT	When working at ground level: — *Don't* kneel — *Do* crawl
WRONG RIGHT	When lying down: — *Don't* let your body curve — *Do* keep your body straight.

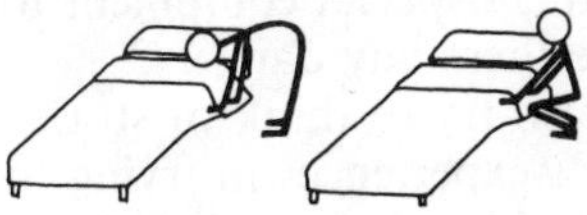

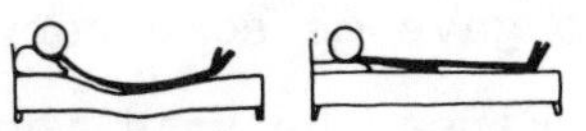

Exercise 3
Guided writing

Imagine your father was the patient. He wrote a letter to his brother, who also has back trouble. Write that letter, following the conversation in Exercise 2, and including all the information. Start like this:

Dear Roger,

I got some very useful advice about my back yesterday. My doctor gave me a chart and told me how to avoid backache. I'm sure this will help you too.

The best thing he said was that ....
.... so I asked him how I should
.... He gave me a chart and said that I should ....

Continue the letter, using expressions like *he advised me to, he warned that, he suggested that, he told me to.*

Exercise 4
Planning a letter

The class divides into pairs. They have to prepare a letter of advice to a cousin who wishes to learn a new language, a new sport, how to drive a car, how to fly an aeroplane or any other suitable activity. Together, they consider questions like:

Is it best to go to a special school or to find a private teacher?
How much will the lessons cost?
How long will it take?
Are there examinations to pass?
Is there special equipment to buy (eg tennis racket, or books)?
Are there any dangers?

They also try to think of stories about their own or imaginary people's experiences in trying to learn the same thing.
They decide on the order in which they would write about these things, and prepare a tidy plan for a letter.

Exercise 5
Free writing

Each pair of students exchange the plan from Exercise 4 with another pair. Still working as a pair, they compose a letter to the cousin in which they report the advice they have received in the other pair's plan.
The letter should start like this:

```
Dear . . . .

   I got your letter asking for advice about
learning . . . .  Actually, I have never learned
. . . . myself, but I asked my friend . . . .,
who gave me some very good ideas.

   First, he said that . . . .
```

Unit 10 Factual and emotive language

Advertisement A

Yugoslavia – and more!

HOLIDAYS IN YUGOSLAVIA–AND NOW GREECE, ROMANIA AND AUSTRIA.

This year, more than ever, is the time to choose Yugotours. Because this year Yugotours offer more countries, more holidays, more service and more value than ever before.

Now we can arrange a variety of exciting holidays in three new countries, each with its own special fascination. Sea and sun holidays, lake and mountain holidays, away-from-it-all islands, coach tours and cruises.

We do more for you!

It's Yugotours expertise and special individual attention that makes a good holiday perfect. We offer the best choice of flights. The greatest selection of resorts. Hotels which are hand-picked to suit every taste–and pocket. And above all, we offer reliability–its the best value around.

Send for your Yugotours brochure now and make your next holiday more of a holiday than ever.

More countries and more seaside lake & mountain holidays, coach tours & cruises than ever before

Yugotours Limited, Head Office,
Chesham House, 150 Regent Street,
London W1R 5FA. Tel: 01-734 7321.
18/20 Booth Street, Manchester M24AN.
Tel: 061-228 6891.

Name ______________________

Address ______________________

____

____

Advertisement B

YUGOSLAVIA

Holidays in Yugoslavia, Greece, Romania and Austria

This year is the time to choose Yugotours. Because this year Yugotours offer four countries, twelve holidays, five different types of service and value for money.

We now arrange different holidays in three new countries. There will be sea and sun, lakes and mountains, lonely islands, coach tours and cruises.

We have experts and we give you individual attention. We have a choice of five flights, and eight holiday resorts. We have inspected all the hotels. None costs more than £40 per night for one person for bed and breakfast. We try very hard to keep to our arrangements with you.

If you write to us, we will send you our brochure.

Exercise 1
Word Study

(i) Which advertisement on page 31 { gives more facts? / sounds more exciting?

(ii) Count the number of times the word *more* appears in advertisement A. Does it appear in advertisement B?

(iii) Count the times the words *good, better, best* appear in advertisement A. Do they appear in advertisement B?

(iv) Find the words *exciting, special fascination, expertise, special, individual attention, perfect, greatest, hand-picked*, in advertisement A. Do they give the reader more facts than in advertisement B? What do they add to the advertisement A?

Exercise 2
Completion

The Express Tours advertisement below is without many exciting words. Choose words from the box and put them into the advertisement instead of the words underlined. Write out the whole advertisement again. If you can think of other exciting words, use them.

paradise, promise you more, promise more than, many more, a huge range of, an enormous number of, exotic, delights, offer, fantastic, the best possible, all this under one roof.

FLY TO <u>ASIA OR AUSTRALIA</u> WITH EXPRESS TOURS.
If you're planning a holiday — or a trip home to Asia or Australia this year — Express Tours can make many <u>different arrangements with you</u>.
We can <u>arrange</u> 13 airlines, including Malaysian Airline System, Quantas, Thai International, and <u>10 others</u>, with <u>40 possible</u> destinations and <u>56</u> departure dates.
If you like staying overnight in <u>non-Western</u> cities like Singapore, Bangkok or Kuala Lumpur for sun, shopping, sightseeing or other Asian <u>activities</u>, we can <u>arrange</u> a <u>useful</u> Reduced Stopover Package that is <u>very cheap</u>.
<u>Write or come to see us</u> at 26 Oxford Road, London S.W.8.

Exercise 3
Understanding

There are different kinds of advertisements. They change according to the people they are written for, and according to the importance of facts. Look at advertisements *A* and *B* opposite.
Answer these questions:

1 What is each advertising?
2 Which advertisement gives facts?
3 In the advertisement that does not give facts, what kind of persuasion is being used? (the picture, strong words ....?)

Exercise 4
Rewriting

Now change each advertisement. Make the factual one more exciting, and make the emotional one more factual (invent facts if you do not have true information). In your emotional advertisement use as many adjectives and adverbs as you can. But remember, advertisements must not be too long.

Advertisement A

Advertisement B

Exercise 5
Free writing

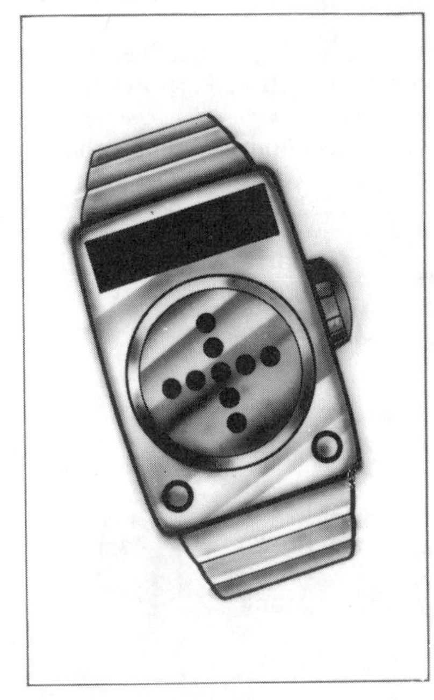

Below is a picture of a wrist-telephone, the WRISTEL. We will probably have such things by 1990 when satellites are built to transmit solar energy (the sun's power) for many new uses. The Wristel will be powered by solar energy from a satellite and will be quite cheap.

Imagine that you have to prepare a page of information about Wristels that are made in the factory where you work. The information is for shopkeepers. You have to influence them to sell Wristels in their shops.

(i) First decide whether you will write a factual or an emotional page, or perhaps a mixture of both.

(ii) Then write the page of information, using headlines and arranging the page nicely with some writing and some illustration. Include information like:

a This is a new invention
b Wristel allows you to talk to anyone in the world at any time
c It costs no money to use Wristel
d Wristel is cheap to buy
e Wristel has been tested for 5 years and is guaranteed against faults
f Wristel is small, light, and comfortable to wear
g Wristel is made by .... (invent the name of a factory) who have a good reputation

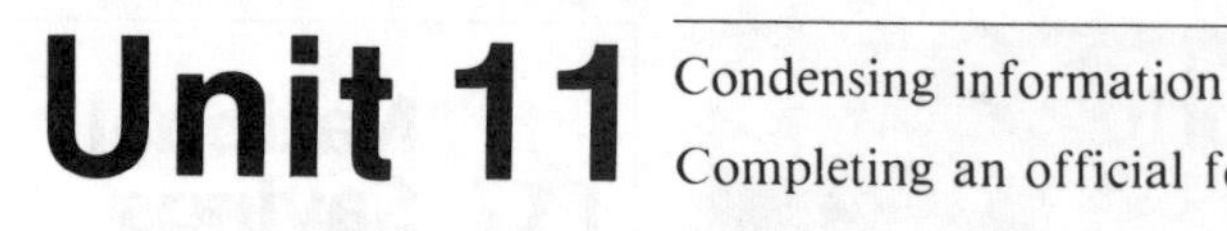

Unit 11

Condensing information

Completing an official form

Giving explanations

Exercise 1
Sentence writing

Sarah Jones flew to Jamaica for a holiday. She lost one suitcase, so she had to fill out a claim form for her insurance company. There was not much space in the form, so she gave the necessary information very briefly, eg

Item
1 pair of shoes
Black
£18
Size 5
high-heeled
party

She means:

I lost one pair of shoes.
The shoes were black.
The shoes cost £18
The shoes were size 5.
The shoes were high-heeled.
The shoes are worn to parties.

These sentences can be joined into one:

I lost one pair of size 5, black, high-heeled party shoes, costing £18.

Joining adjectives in a row usually means using this order:

size	*age*	*colour*	*participle*	*place or material or other specific detail*	*use*	*NOUN*
size 5		black	high-heeled		party	shoes
small	new	green	folding	silk		umbrella

Note We normally have no more than two or three adjectives. Only special writing like an official form, or an advertisement, uses long rows of adjectives.

Use this information to write seven sentences about the things that Sarah lost.

1 jacket
red
£35
velvet
new

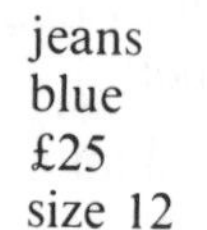

2 jeans
blue
£25
size 12

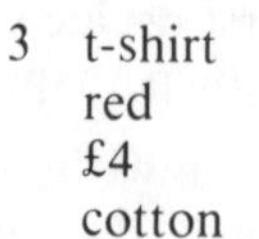

3 t-shirt
red
£4
cotton

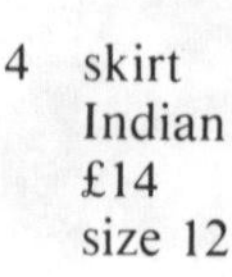

4 skirt
Indian
£14
size 12

5 towel
red/white
£5
large
striped
beach

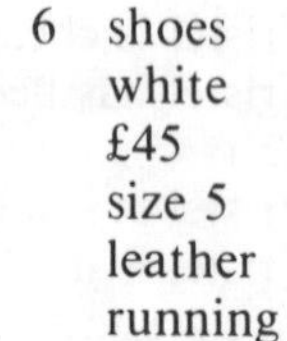

6 shoes
white
£45
size 5
leather
running

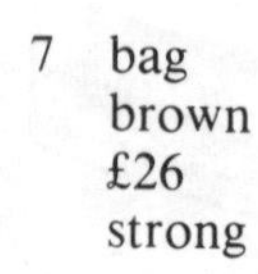

7 bag
brown
£26
strong

Exercise 2
Guided sentences

Imagine yourself with the same problem as Sarah. Make a list of items lost and then fill out this claim form to an insurance company. Use at least three adjectives to describe every lost item.

CLAIM FORM

Surname Mr/Mrs/Miss/Ms ______________________________

Forenames (*Underline the main one*) ______________________________

Date of journey ______________________________

Date of return ______________________________

Flight number ______________________________

Destination ______________________________

Point of departure ______________________________

Permanent address ______________________________

Brief description of articles lost, including cost ______________________________

____

____

Signature ______________________ Date ______________________

Exercise 3
Adjective order

Make as many groups of *three* adjectives (in the right order) as you can before each of the nouns.

clean, sterilised, cotton,
gauze, sharp, new, small,
large, soft, white, washed
useful, protective, long, rolled.

Noun
bandage
scissors
handkerchief

Exercise 4
Adverb order

When more than one adverbial follows a verb, the most common order is the one in this table. Use it to write (i) six sensible sentences containing three adverbials and (ii) two amusing (not sensible) sentences containing three adverbials.

Verb	Adverbial of manner	Adverbial of place	Adverbial of time
Place a bandage	quickly	on the table	when you can
Stand the vase	carefully	in the dryer	as soon as possible
Dry the pullover	gently	over the wound	before you leave
Clean the car	completely	into the goal	after washing it
Kick the ball	thoroughly	all over	on Saturday
Mow the lawn	properly	on the outside	this afternoon

Exercise 5
Guided writing

Your school is going on a camping holiday and you are in charge of the medical preparations. One person must take a *First Aid Kit.* Use the following information to:

What you need in a kit		
	Padded Bandage medium Sterilised Gauze large	2 2
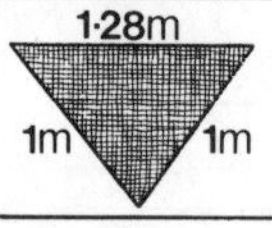	Triangluar Bandage strong, cotton	2
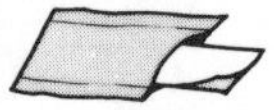	Tissue Wipes wet, prepared	10
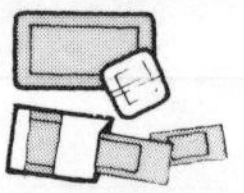	Adhesive Plasters soft, assorted sizes, waterproof	20
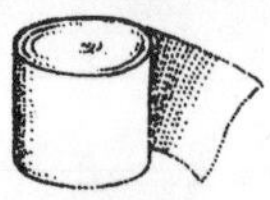	Stretch Bandages (715 cm) firm, white	2
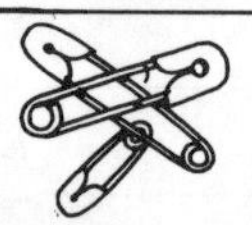	Safety Pins reliable, rustproof, varied, steel	12
	Scissors stainless steel, sharp, small	1 pair
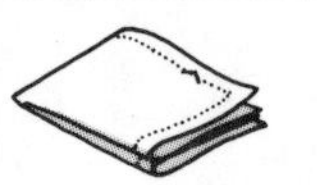	Handkerchief cotton, white, clean	1
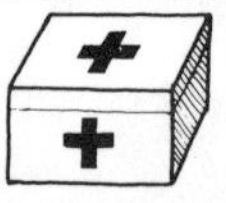	Box plastic, dry, light	1

(i) write a description of things to buy for the *First Aid Kit.* Write a series of nine notes, following the chart. The first is done for you:
1 two medium padded bandages, and two large sterilised gauze bandages.

(ii) write a page of explanation about what to do after an accident. Write sentences using the seven items of information below. In each case, join the first two sentences into one, starting 'You should. . . .' Then join the next three sentences into one, so that you have one sentence with two or three adverbials at the end. (*Note:* you may have to change some adjectives to adverbs.) The first two are done for you:

In case of accidents:

1 *For bleeding wounds.* They need protection against dirt. Place a padded bandage over the wound. Be careful. Do this as soon as possible.

You should protect bleeding wounds against dirt. Place a padded bandage **carefully over the wound as soon as possible.**

MANNER | PLACE | TIME

2 *For small cuts.* They need covering. Stick a plaster across the wound. You must be exact. Do it after choosing the right size.

You should cover small cuts. Stick a plaster exactly across the wound after choosing the right size.

3 *For broken arms.* They need supporting. Make a sling. Make the sling for the whole arm. Be gentle but firm.

4 *For open wounds.* They need cleaning. Wipe the wound. Be thorough. Do this after washing your own hands.

5 *For strained muscles.* They need supporting. Keep a bandage around the leg or arm. You must be firm. Keep it there until the swelling disappears.

6 *For bleeding.* It needs stopping. Press the sides of the wound together. You must be quick. You must also be very firm.

7 *For a person suffering from cold.* This person needs warming. Wrap the person in a coat or blanket. Wrap him/her completely. Do this after finding shelter from wind or rain.

Unit 12

Revision

Comparing past with present habits

Because of this to refer back

Exercise 1

There was a transport strike in New York a little while ago. No one could use the buses or the subway. However, people still came to work. Look at this short radio report about the strike.

Note: Subway = underground train
Jogging = slow running

The strike has changed New York. It's 8 o'clock in the morning, and we can see legs everywhere. Instead of taking a bus or a train, more than one million people are marching, jogging, or just walking down the roads to work. An army of cyclists is pedalling into the business district. Several hundred people are on roller-skates, and one man is on a horse! Usually there are one million cars and lorries on Manhattan's roads, but today there are close to two million.

Because of this, New York is a different city.

To show a change we can join two sentences using *but*, and show a contrast with an adverb:

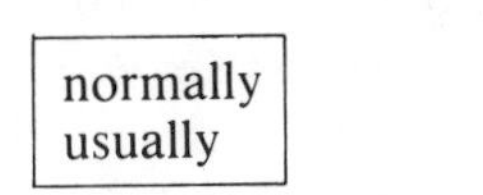

today
now
this morning
yesterday
last week
tomorrow

eg Tom travels to work by bus.
Tom is walking.

Tom *usually* travels to work by bus, *but today* he is walking.
yesterday he walked.
tomorrow he will walk.

Joining sentences

(i) Join these sentences to describe a change. Put the verbs in the correct tense:

a Sandra (drive) to work. Sandra (cycle).
b Bill and Oliver (play) football on Fridays. Bill and Oliver (go) swimming.
c Dennis (watch) TV every night. Dennis (go) to evening class.

Guided writing

(ii) Use the ideas in the radio talk to write seven more sentences.

Exercise 2
Writing paragraphs

A newspaper reporter interviewed some New Yorkers during the strike. She asked them how they came to work. Then she used her notes to write about them. This is one paragraph she wrote:

Tom Fox is a shopkeeper in the city. He usually travels to work by bus, but during the strike he walks and arrives ten minutes earlier! Tom hates the rain and people roller-skating. However, he likes the exercise. Tom's mornings are better now. Because of this, he doesn't mind the strike.

Use these notes to write three similar paragraphs about these people:

NAME	Ann Grimes	Michael Hardy	Jason Edwards
WORK	engineer	businessman	student
TRAVEL *usual*	bus/1 hour	train/45 mins	train/30 mins
now	bicycle/30 mins	car/1½ hr	roller-skates/50 mins
HATES	dogs and lorries	traffic and long time	banana skins and people in the way
LIKES	speed and exercise	the radio in the car	movement of the roller-skates

Note: Because of this: The word *this* can mean one or more things that you have already mentioned.

Exercise 3
Comparative sentences

Bob Ferguson weighs 80 kg. He is 1.75 m. tall. His wife Jean weighs 62 kg. She is 1.57 m. tall. They are both overweight (= too fat). This is a chart of what they usually eat every day. The numbers after the foods are the calories. If people eat too many calories, they get fat. Bob and Jean eat nearly 5000 calories every day.

8 am		11 am		1 pm	
Breakfast		*Morning tea*		*Lunch*	
fried egg	132	1 cup of tea or coffee		chicken pie	385
bacon	128	with milk	20	chips	400
sausage	140	and sugar	12	jam tart	229
3 slices of toast	210	6 biscuits or 1 bun	200	crisps	134
butter	80			coffee with milk	20
marmalade	35			and sugar	12
2 cups of tea					
with milk	40				
and sugar	26				
	791		232		1180

CHICKEN PIE | JAM TART | CRISPS | Plate of 2 PORK CHOPS, 2 ROAST POTATOES, FRIED MUSHROOMS | BOWL OF CEREAL AND MILK | TOMATO AND ONION SALAD

4 pm		7 pm		10 pm	
Afternoon tea		*Dinner*		*Supper*	
1 cup of tea with milk	20	Cream of tomato soup	200	dry biscuits	80
and sugar	12	2 pork chops	1020	cheese	210
1 bar of chocolate or		2 roast potatoes	140	milk cocoa	160
cake	335	fried mushrooms	125		
		fruit salad and cream	180		
		beer or wine	115		
	367		1780		450

The following chart shows a better diet:
(*Note:* your *diet* is the food you normally eat.
to go on a diet means to eat less in order to lose weight.)

Breakfast		*Morning tea*		*Lunch*	
bowl of cereal with milk		tea or coffee (no milk or		fish	180
and sugar	200	sugar)		tomato and onion salad	90
1 slice of toast	83	1 small cake or 3 biscuits	85	1 orange	40
1 apple	40			water	
tea or coffee					
(no milk or sugar)					
	323		85		310
Afternoon tea		*Dinner*		*Supper*	
tea or coffee		chicken	215	fruit	100
(no milk or sugar)		carrot salad	25	fruit juice	50
1 small cake or 3 biscuits	85	rice	143		
		1 banana	67		
		tea or coffee (no milk or			
		sugar)			
	85		450		150

(i) When we compare two things we can use:
more
or *less* + adjective + *than*

eg Bob is more overweight than Jean. Jean is less overweight than Bob. Dinner is more fattening than lunch. Lunch is less fattening than dinner.

Note: Fattening foods make you fat.

Compare Bob and Jean's usual meals with the better diet and use the information to write 3 sentences with *more fattening than*, 3 sentences with *less fattening than*.

(ii) When we compare two things we can also use:

more
or *less* + noun + *than*
or *fewer*

eg Bob's usual breakfast has more calories than the new breakfast.
The new breakfast has less fattening food than Bob's usual breakfast.
The new breakfast has fewer calories than Bob's usual breakfast.

Use the information in the charts to write 3 sentences with *more* .... *than*, 3 sentences with *less* .... *than*, and 3 sentences with *fewer* .... *than*.

Exercise 4
Writing paragraphs

(i) Bob and Jean Ferguson talked to a dietician (a person who gives advice about a diet, usually in a hospital) and she said, 'You normally eat very fattening meals. Because of this, you are overweight. This means you must eat less from now on.'
Use the information in the charts in Exercise 3 to write the dietician's hospital report about the Fergusons.

a Use her notes for paragraph 1:

Bob F. h. 1.75 wt. 80
Jean F. 1.57 62
Came because overweight.
Should eat less — 1300 cals. max.
Normally eat 4000+ cals. a day.

(max. = maximum)
(+ = more than)

b For paragraph 2 use the information in the charts to choose food for the Fergusons and make suggestions for breakfast, lunch and dinner. Use expressions like:
They should eat ....
Less fattening foods for breakfast are ....
Lunch should have less than .... calories. Because of this .... and .... and .... or .... would be a good idea.
They should avoid .... for dinner, because .... very fattening.

(ii) Bob and Jean Ferguson are on a month's diet. Write three sentences to compare what they usually eat with what they eat while on a diet. Use sentences like those in Exercise 1.

Exercise 5
Free writing

Discuss the difference between English foods and the foods you normally eat. Then write a short essay explaining:

(i) the difference between English foods and the foods you have for breakfast, lunch, etc.

(ii) your views about the best foods to eat.

Unit 13

Note-taking

Logical arrangement of information

Writing summaries

Exercise 1
Paragraph arrangement

Newspapers use headlines to help their readers. Here are three headlines and eight paragraphs from a newspaper story.
(a) Decide what order the paragraphs should have. The middle three (4, 5, 6) are already numbered for you.
(b) Decide which is the main headline, and where the other two should go. (There is more than one possible arrangement.)

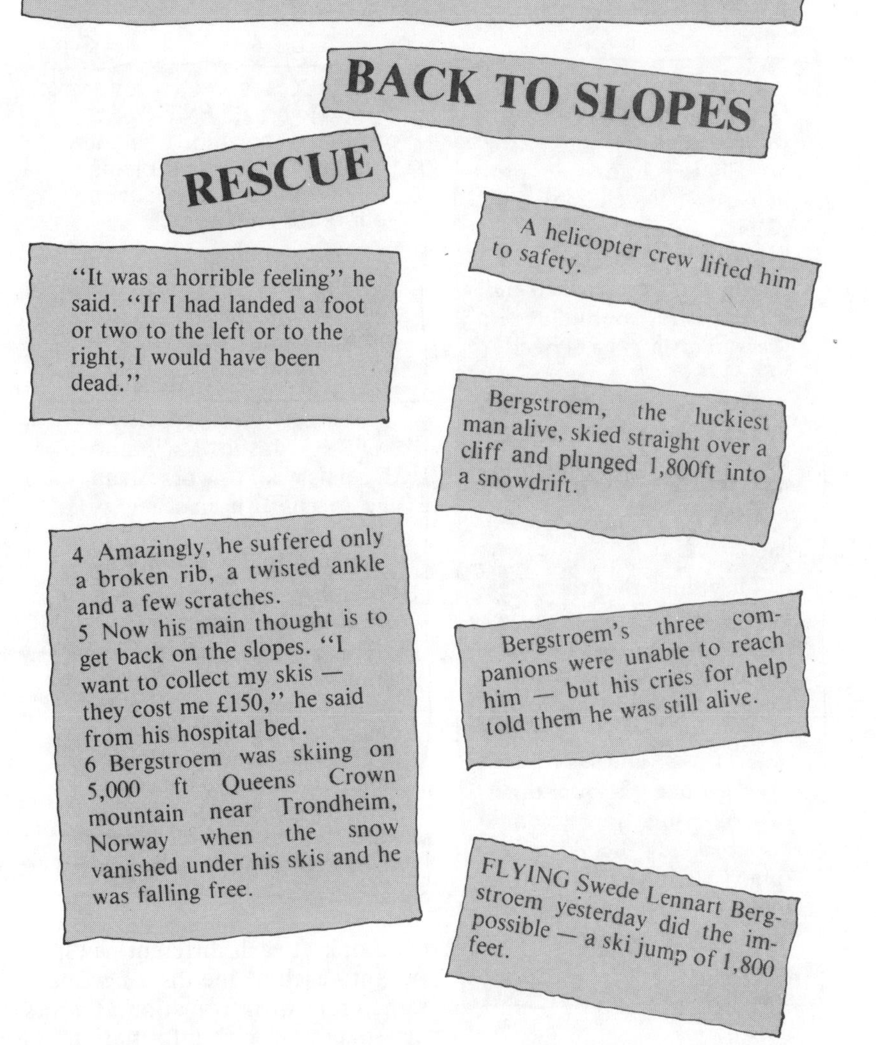

ALIVE! THE SPACE TRIP SKIER

BACK TO SLOPES

RESCUE

A helicopter crew lifted him to safety.

"It was a horrible feeling" he said. "If I had landed a foot or two to the left or to the right, I would have been dead."

Bergstroem, the luckiest man alive, skied straight over a cliff and plunged 1,800ft into a snowdrift.

4 Amazingly, he suffered only a broken rib, a twisted ankle and a few scratches.
5 Now his main thought is to get back on the slopes. "I want to collect my skis — they cost me £150," he said from his hospital bed.
6 Bergstroem was skiing on 5,000 ft Queens Crown mountain near Trondheim, Norway when the snow vanished under his skis and he was falling free.

Bergstroem's three companions were unable to reach him — but his cries for help told them he was still alive.

FLYING Swede Lennart Bergstroem yesterday did the impossible — a ski jump of 1,800 feet.

(c) Write out the story, with the headlines, in the right order.

Exercise 2
Guided writing

Different newspapers often include different facts in the stories they write about the same event. They also arrange facts in different ways. Here are three newspapers' stories about the same event.

(i) Combine all the facts from each newspaper to make one complete story. Follow the headlines in the order given. You can have one or more paragraphs under each headline.

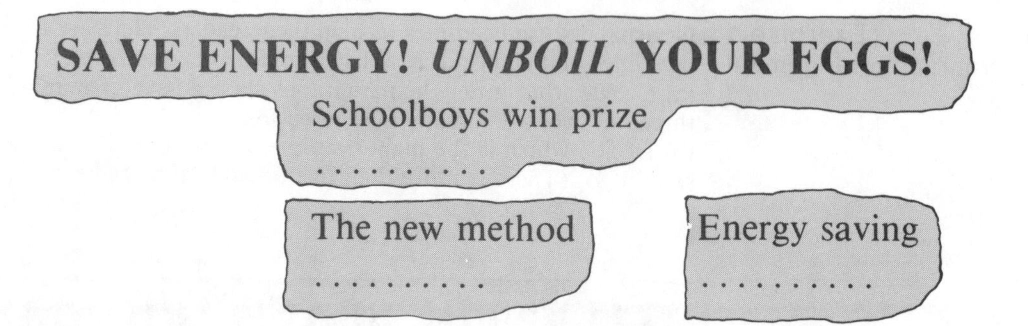

Jason Lacy, Richard Goulding and Ian South, three second formers at the Sir Charles Lucas comprehensive school, claim that by placing an egg in cold water, bringing it to the boil, taking it off the cooker and leaving it for six minutes in the water, you get a perfectly-boiled egg.

They entered their method in the national energy saving competition for schools. They have won £50 for their school, and £5 each.

They think that their idea could save £3 million in fuel bills if everyone were to start cooling eggs for six minutes instead of boiling them for four.

Jason, 12, said last night: "We've done it a lot of times to make sure, and it comes out properly boiled every time." He did not learn the method from his mother, "but she does it that way now."

- LITTLE Jason Lacey, 12, and two pals have won a prize for solving one of Britain's energy problems — £3 million spent each year on boiling eggs.
- After working out the heat loss, the boys invented the perfect "four-minute" egg without the wasted energy.
- Place the eggs in boiling water, turn off the heat and leave for six minutes.
- Their eggcellent idea won Jason and classmates Richard Goulding and Ian South £65 from Essex County Council.

YOUNG Jason Lacy and two pals went to work on an egg to cut Britain's energy bill.

They found a better way of boiling one and won a prize for their idea.

The boys decided that the nation wastes gas or electricity worth £3 million a year by boiling eggs the old way.

They did some experiments and found this save-it method:

Lower the egg into boiling water, turn off the heat at once and leave for six minutes.

Jason, of Antonio Way, Colchester, Essex, said "Our method gives exactly the same result as boiling an egg for four minutes."

"The yolk is perfect and the white neither runny nor hard".

Jason, 12, and his schoolmates Richard Goulding and Ian South, both 13, won the £65 first prize in a "save energy" contest run by Essex County Council.

The boys got £5 each and the rest of the cash went to their school, the Sir Charles Lucas comprehensive at Colchester.

(ii) Look at each different newspaper. What headings could you put into each of the three newspapers? Do any of them follow the same order of information as yours? Why, in your opinion, does a newspaper *not* give information in logical order? Do you think newspapers should be more logical?

Exercise 3 Summarising

This is a story about burglars in England.

(i) As you read it, make a note in one or two words of the main point of every paragraph.
(ii) Then use your notes to arrange the information in a logical way to suit the main headline: **TWO BOXING MEN ROBBED,** and write a very short account of the main points (about seven sentences).

Boxing referee, James Pattison, has been robbed twice by thieves! While he was refereeing at the Park Centre, Horsham, his car was stolen. Police found it a few days later but without tools and other things worth £250.

He spent the day working on the car and in the evening went with his family to watch a football match. They returned at 9.30 pm to find thieves had burgled their Pankhurst Avenue, Brighton, home. Gold and silver jewellery was missing from his wife Betty's and daughter Julie's rooms.

'I don't think it was worth much', he said. 'It had sentimental value. The thieves got in through a back window I left open and ruined the three bedrooms. I'm not feeling very lucky at the moment. A few days ago a machine at my factory broke down, so now I can't do my job properly.'

A policeman said there was no link between the burglary at the Pattison's home and that in boxing promoter Paddy O'Connor's home recently. Thieves raided Mr O'Connor's home while he was at a boxing evening at Hove Town Hall. Jewellery worth £3,000 was taken.

'I don't think this latest burglary means somebody is going round the homes of local boxers when they know they will be out. This just seems to have been an ordinary burglary,' said the policeman.

Exercise 4 Now do the same as in Exercise 3 with this story. The main headline is: **DOG LEAVES ARMY**

The Army's favourite dog of war was given a soldier's farewell yesterday.

Rats, the terrier who braved bombs and bullets with the troops, flew to retirement. He was brought back by soldiers returning from a tour of duty abroad and was given a special retirement parade at their barracks in London yesterday.

No one is certain when Rats first wandered into the army barracks but he has accompanied at least ten different regiments there. During that time he has been fired on, wounded on two occasions by car bombs and twice hit by cars. He still carries four bullets inside him.

Now, at eight years old, his health is beginning to suffer too much for him to stay on active duty.

Exercise 5 Go back to Exercise 1 and Exercise 2, and write a very brief summary of each story — about three sentences.

Unit 14

Letters, asking for or giving advice, or making suggestions
Paragraph planning

Many newspapers and magazines have an *Agony Column*. 'Agony' means pain, but an *Agony Column* has letters asking for and giving advice.

Exercise 1
Matching exercise

(i) Read these letters and match them. There are three pairs.

a

Dear Helpful,

My husband and I have been married for about one year, and we still cannot decide how often we should visit our parents. Can you advise us what to do? My husband's parents and mine live about a half an hour away from us. Unfortunately, we are very busy and can only visit them every four to six weeks. They are all complaining. They say we should spend more time with them. Do you think we should see them more often? Guilty.

b

Dear Helpful,

This is my problem. Have you any suggestions? A few months ago, I met a very nice boy. He normally sees me once a week, but yesterday he told me that he had another girlfriend. Nevertheless, he still wants to see me every week. But I can't decide. If you were me, what would you do? Confused.

c

Dear Helpful,

I work very hard in my job and have little time for pleasure. I go out with a girl sometimes. Her parents are friendly with my parents. Recently I discovered that they think I should marry her. I don't want to marry her, but I don't want to make her unhappy. Have you any suggestions? Worried.

d

Dear .....

[1]I understand your difficulty. [2]You must remain friendly with the girl's family because of your parents. [3]On the other hand, you must show them that you do not wish to marry her. [4]The best I can suggest is that you go out with the girl less often, and that you also go out with other girls. [5]You could sometimes mention the other girls to her. [6]This would show that you do not wish to marry yet.

e

Dear .....

[1]Frequent visits to parents can be difficult. [2]However, you should remember that your parents are your best friends, and that they deserve your friendship. [3]I would advise you to understand their loneliness. [4]Moreover, one day, perhaps when you have a baby, you will need their help. [5]In my opinion, you should at least telephone or write to them once a week, and visit them every two to three weeks.

f

Dear .....

[1]You are fond of the boy, but you want his respect. [2]I suggest that you explain your feelings to him. [3]Say that you like him and that you are hurt by the idea of the other girlfriend. [4]If he is really fond of you, he will give up the other girl. [5]If not, you are wasting your time with him. [6]If I were you, I would ask myself: [7]Is this the right boy for me? [8]He seems rather weak. [9]He can't decide what he wants.

(ii) Find these expressions in the letters and underline them.

What do you think I should do?
Should I ....?
Do you think I should ....?
Can you advise me what to do?
Have you any suggestions?
If you were me, what would you do?

In my opinion, you should ....
I would advise you to ....
I suggest that you (+ infinitive) ....
All / The best } I can suggest is that you (+ infinitive) ....
If I were you, I would ....
You could ....

Completion (iii) Complete the answer to Miserable overleaf:

Dear Helpful,

My life at school is ruined by two boys who bully me all the time. It is a new school for me, and my mother thinks I love it, but I don't. It's terrible. The two bullies even follow me on the way to school and laugh at my clothes. Once they deliberately spilled a drink over me. I am usually a friendly person, but now I am so unhappy that I can't make friends. What should I do? Miserable.

(*Note:* You will need the word *therefore*,)

g

Dear Miserable,

[1]This is a common situation. [2]You are new.... school, and can't.... friends to support you. [3]If you tell the teacher, things could get worse.[4] But you can.... your classmates. [5].... I suggest.... you talk.... some of your classmates about the bullies. [6]If they know...., they will stop. [7]If I.... you, I.... get a lot of friends on your side.

Exercise 2
Paragraph plans

Look back at the replies in Exercise 1. Each one follows the three parts of the plan below. Use the numbers of the sentences in each reply to show which sentences belong to each part of the plan.

PLAN	REPLY **d**	REPLY **e**	REPLY **f**	REPLY **g**
Comment about the problem				
Some advice				
Final, main point				

Exercise 3
Free writing

Write a reply to this letter, following the plan in Exercise 2.

Dear Helpful,

I'm a nervous seventeen-year-old who wears very thick glasses. Two years ago, a boy I liked laughed at me because of my glasses. Recently, I went out with a nice boy, but I still felt unattractive. After a while, he dropped me. I can't get contact lenses. I'm very miserable. What can I do? Unloved.

Dear Unloved ....

Exercise 4
Free writing

A recent letter to an agony column described the problems of a left-handed person. It received an encouraging reply because there are many left-handed people (left-handers). Do the test and then use the information to write *both* letters.

Common problems for left-handers

1 People think they are clumsy.
2 People think they are less intelligent.
3 People think they are slow.
4 They cannot use scissors easily.
5 They cannot use a tin-opener easily.
6 They cannot use a potato-peeler easily.
7 They cannot use a pen easily.
8 It is difficult to write from left to right.

A test

How left-handed are you?

For each of the following:
Put a ✓ for the hand you prefer to use;
and a ✓✓ where your preference is so strong that you'd never use the other hand unless absolutely forced to.

If it really doesn't matter to you which hand you use, put a ✓ in both columns.

Now add up the ✓ in each column .... *Total:*	......	......
Put the smaller number under the larger and subtract it .... *Result:*	...... **OR**	......
Add up *all* the ✓ in both columns, and divide the Result by this number:	...... **OR**	......
Multiply the answer by 10.	...... **OR**	......

You should get a number between 0 and 10. If it's in the left column, you tend to be left-handed; if in the right column, you tend to be right-handed. The higher the number you get, the more left- or right-handed you are. The most common left- or right-handed score is about 8. If you get a figure of 0, you'd seem to be ambidextrous.

LEFT HAND		RIGHT HAND
	WRITING	
	DRAWING	
	THROWING	
	SCISSORS	
	TOOTHBRUSH	
	KNIFE (without fork)	
	SPOON	
	BROOM which is the upper hand?	
	STRIKING HAND which hand holds match?	
	OPENING BOX which hand opens lid?	

Test derived from work by R C Oldfield, MRC Speech and Communication Research Unit, University of Edinburgh Which? Oct. 1979

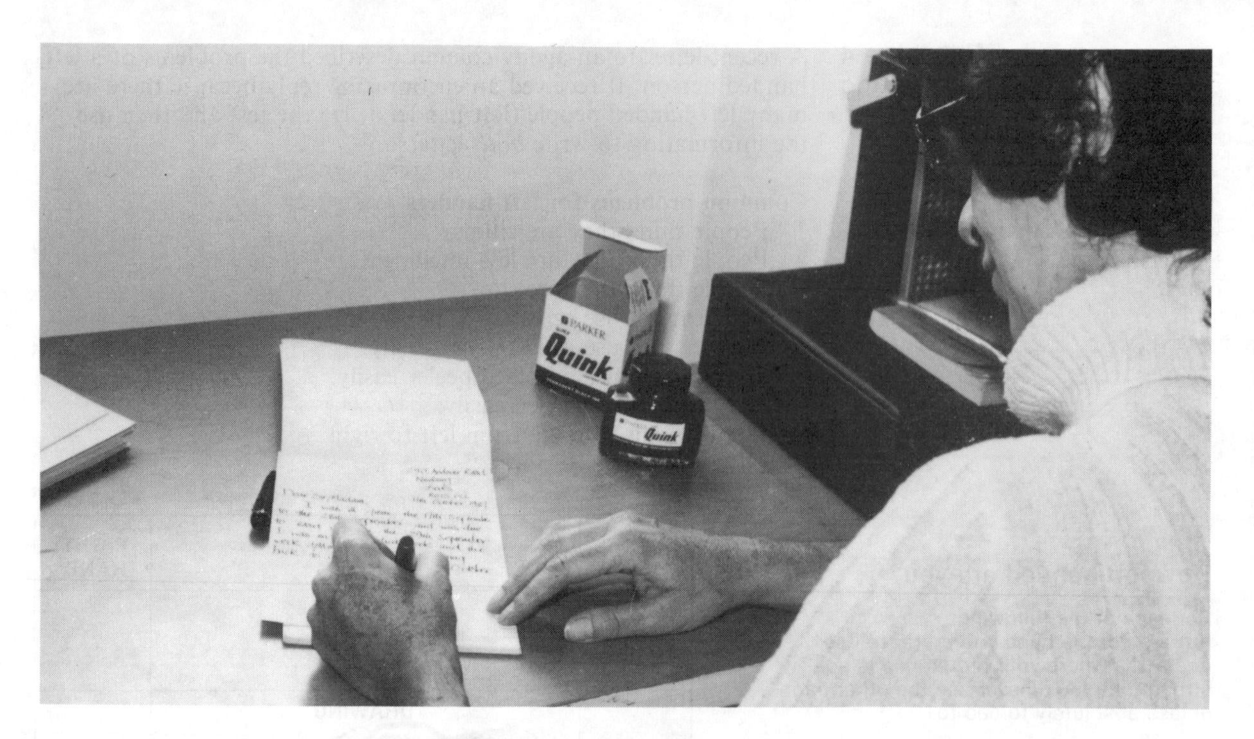

Help

1 Parents and teachers are less strict about using the right hand (In earlier times, they forced children to use the right hand.)
2 There are famous left-handers in sport.
3 A left-hander can do most things as well as a right-handed person.
4 You can buy left-handed scissors, tin-openers, pens, etc.
5 For writing, a left-hander should:
   — sit on the right side of the table, with the paper on the left. (The arm can move freely this way)
   — turn the paper at an angle.
   — use a soft pencil, a smooth ball-point, or a flexible pen.

Exercise 5
Writing game

Form small groups in the class and make a list of problems.
Working as a group, write a letter asking Helpful for advice about one of them.
Exchange letters with another group, and, still working as a group, write the reply.

Unit 15

Classifying information

Report writing from notes

Exercise 1
Letter planning

When you write a letter of application for a job, you should include the information that the employer needs.

(i) Look at this list, and put a ✓ against the important information:

1 age
2 married or single
3 address
4 parents' job(s)
5 height
6 name
7 qualifications for this job
8 hobbies
9 male or female
10 what job you want
11 name of school
12 likes and dislikes
13 number of brothers and sisters
14 colour of eyes and hair
15 education
16 past or present job(s)
17 names of one or two people who can recommend you
18 why you want this job

(ii) Arrange the items you have ticked in logical groups, such as 'personal details', 'education', etc.

Exercise 2
Understanding

Jane wants to become a nurse. She intends to write to a training hospital. Look at these three letters and decide which one is best. Discuss your reasons, and suggest improvements if you can.

10 Hunter's Close
Bradford

14 February 1983

The Matron
St Bride's Hospital
Newton Abbot
Devon

Dear Madam

I would like to apply for a student nurse training job to start in August, 1984.

I am seventeen years old and am studying for my final exams in biology, chemistry, and geography.

I would be grateful if you could send me information and application forms.

Yours faithfully

Jane Walker

Jane Walker

10 Hunter's Close
Bradford

14 February 1983

The Matron
St Bride's Hospital
Newton Abbot
Devon

Dear Mrs Grantham

My name is Jane Walker, and I want to become a nurse.

I am seventeen years old and go to Kingsmead Comprehensive School. Please send me some forms.

Yours sincerely

Jane Walker

Jane Walker

10 Hunter's Close
Bradford

14 February 1983

The Matron
St Bride's Hospital
Newton Abbot
Devon

Dear Matron

I am interested in working in a hospital with sick people. I always watch hospital programmes on TV. My mother is a nurse and I would like to become one as well.

Yours

Jane

Jane

Exercise 3
Planned free writing

Below are some advertisements for jobs in England. The class divides into five groups. Each group prepares full details for a good reply to one of them and, still working as a group, plans and writes a letter of application. These are some ways of starting the letter:

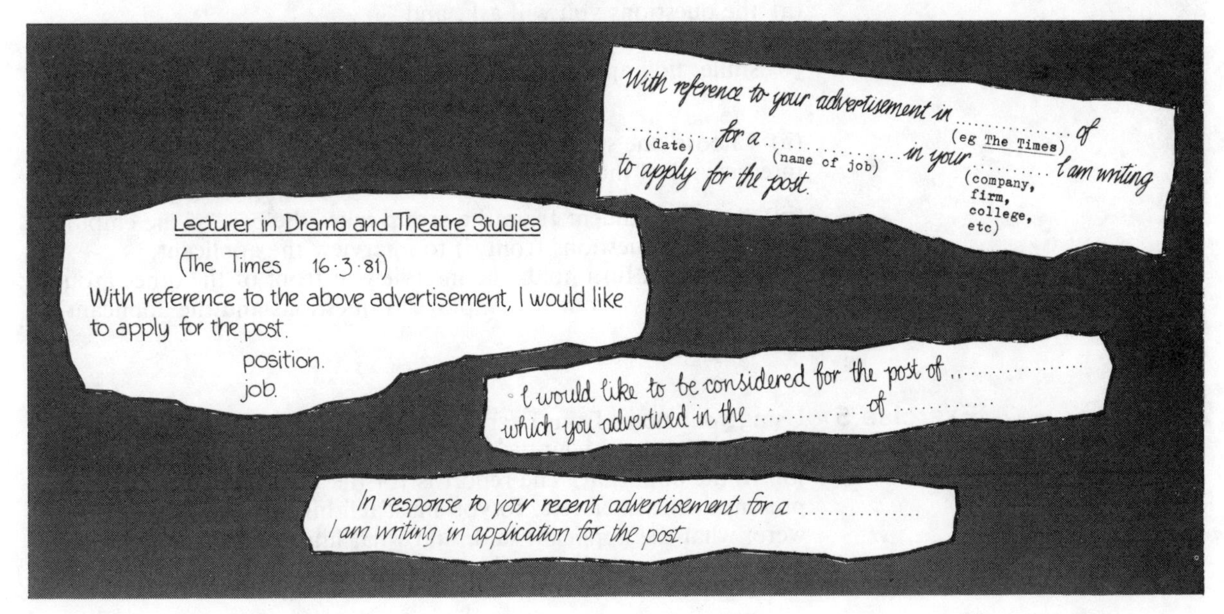

These are some endings for the letters:

I look forward to hearing from you.
Thank you.
If you require any further details, I will be glad to supply them.
A stamped, addressed envelope is enclosed.

CARPENTER'S APPRENTICE

Applications are invited for apprenticeships in carpentry. Applicants should be between 16-24 and interested in woodwork.
Apply: Registrar
Middlesex Polytechnic
48 Wigan Street
LONDON SW2

YOUNG AND ATTRACTIVE WAITRESSES m/f

required for new restaurant in Kensington.
Excellent wages and conditions.
Please telephone 938 1924 between 11 a.m. and 6 p.m. or write to the Manager The Round Table, 14 Pack St., Kensington

ROYAL HOLLOWAY COLLEGE

(University of London)
Egham Hill, Egham,
Surrey TW20 0EX

LECTURER IN DRAMA AND THEATRE STUDIES

Applications are invited for the post of Lecturer tenable from 1st October. Candidates should have a special interest in television drama and film, with research interests in any period of drama.

Salary according to experience.

Applications (2 copies please) to Mrs D. J. Shaw, Personnel Officer.

SECRETARY TOP SALARY

American shipping company in Knightsbridge seeks a secretary with shorthand, to assist the UK Area Manager and Sales Manager. This is a super job for a competent, lively person with secretarial experience. Fringe benefits include pension fund & LVs.

Telephone Margaret Ramage on 586 3499 for Interview.

TEACHER

required, international primary school, Rome, Italy. Minimum two years' experience.

Telephone Harley 861362 for interview immediately or write to K. Evans, 18 Russell St Wigan.

Exercise 4
Note taking

(The class is still working in groups.)

(i) Imagine you are the employer who has received the letter in Exercise 3. and that you want to interview the applicant. Make brief notes of:

(a) the questions you will ask, and
(b) what points you will look for, eg pleasant behaviour, friendly smile, tidy appearance, etc.

(ii) Choose one student in the group to be the applicant at the interview. Tell the 'applicant' how to behave and what to say.

(iii) Another student from the group takes the part of the employer and uses his questions from (i) to interview the applicant.
Each group in turn holds the interview in front of the other groups who take notes about the employer's questions and the applicant's answers.

Exercise 5
Planned free writing

Using your notes from Exercise 4 (iii), write a report about the interview, and say why the company should (or should not) give the job to the applicant. The report is for the Director, who was not present at the interview, so you must tell him what the questions were, what the applicant said, and what impression the applicant gave. Arrange your report in a clear, logical way.

Unit 16

Presenting explanations and opinions
Planning an essay

Exercise 1
Paragraph writing

Some people believe that *Numerology* shows people's character. First, they find a number for every letter of the name, according to this chart.

1	*2*	*3*	*4*	*5*	*6*	*7*	*8*	*9*
a	b	c	d	e	f	g	h	i
j	k	l	m	n	o	p	q	r
s	t	u	v	w	x	y	z	

Mrs Thatcher

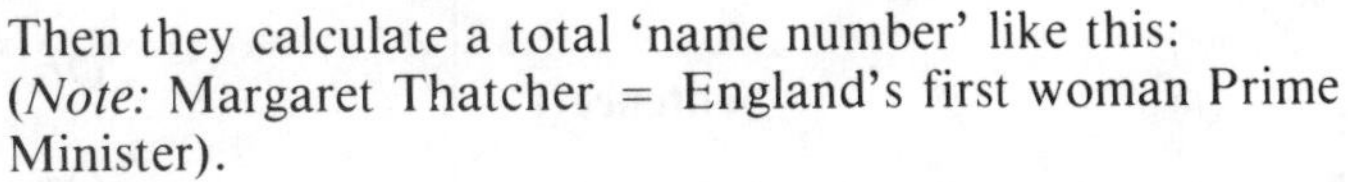

Then they calculate a total 'name number' like this:
(*Note:* Margaret Thatcher = England's first woman Prime Minister).

M A R G A R E T	T H A T C H E R
4+1+9+7+1+9+5+2	2+8+1+2+3+8+5+9
= 38	= 38
3+8 = 11	3+8 = 11
1+1 = 2	1+1 = 2

2+2 = 4

Finally, they find the meaning of that number, as given below.

Numerology
Each number from one to nine has its own meaning:

1 Likes to command, reform, and dominate. More interested in career than home life. May find happiness in later life. Men are frightened of this kind of woman who often marries a weak, loving man. Is practical, clever with money, and can change plans when necessary.
2 Likes to organise. Understands what people want. Emotional, intelligent and confident. Can be jealous and very religious. Prefers work to family, but may become a saint. Often has a career in literature or the arts.
3 Happy, easy to live with. Enjoys hard work. Can command without making people angry. Very successful at work and at home.
4 Wants to rule the world. Enjoys controlling people. Usually feels superior to husband or wife. Is not afraid of power.
5 Longs to help others. Has a warm heart. Is often unhappy at work and lets others take control. But is very good in work that helps other people.
6 Very relaxed. Does not get upset. Works easily with men or women. Makes good friends. May be a writer or an actor.
7 Rather passive. Dreams a lot instead of doing things. Often feels self-pity and makes his or her family angry.
8 Very clever, warm and generous. Popular at home and at work. May over-protect his or her children. Women of this type are both very feminine and very successful. May be a journalist, designer, or public speaker.
9 Either very clever or very silly with money. Full of energy. Often a good driver, sportsman, scientist or businessman.

(i) Work out your own 'name number' and exchange 'name numbers' with another student.

(ii) Write a short paragraph about the other student, taking information from Numerology.
Note: The Numerology meanings are written in note form. Make complete sentences, and link or join sentences wherever possible, using *and*, *but*, *with*, *also*, *in addition*, etc.
(iii) Get the paragraph about yourself back from the other student, and write another paragraph saying whether the description is correct or not. Follow this plan:

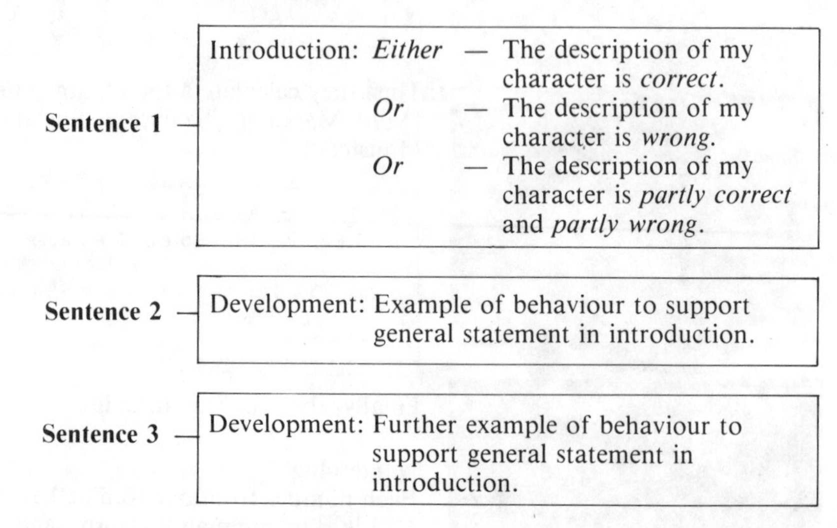

Exercise 2
Rewriting

There are many superstitions in Britain. People believe that certain things will bring them good luck and other things will bring bad luck.

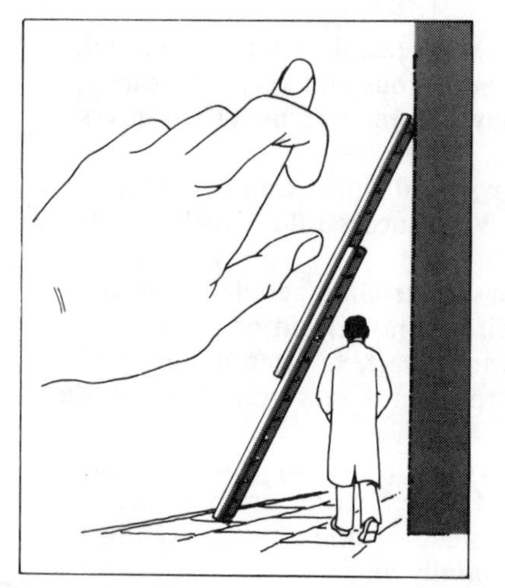

(i) Each of the following sentences is about a superstition. Re-write the sentences in the same way as the first example.

1 If you walk under a ladder, you will have bad luck.
  Walking under a ladder *is* unlucky.
2 If you open an umbrella indoors, you will have bad luck.
3 If you drop a pair of scissors, you will have bad luck.
4 If you see a pin and pick it up, you will have good luck.
5 If you carry a rabbit's foot with you, you will have good luck.
6 If you break a mirror, you will have bad luck for seven years.
7 If you cross your fingers, you will have good luck.
8 If you say 'Touch wood' or 'Knock on wood' while touching some wood, nothing will go wrong with your plans.

(ii) Re-write each of the following sentences in the same way as the first example:

1 If you have a red ear, somebody is talking about you. *Having* a red ear *means that* somebody is talking about you.
2 If you have an itch on the palm of your hand, you will get some money.
3 If you go back home to fetch something that you forgot, an accident could happen to you while you are out.
4 If you see a black cat crossing the street in front of you, you will have good luck.

5 If you eat oysters in a month that has no 'r' in its name, you will lose something.
6 If you step on a crack in the pavement, an accident could happen to your mother.

(iii) Re-write each of your sentences from (i) and (ii) in the past tense, reported speech, eg:
From (i): *People used to believe that* walking under a ladder *was* unlucky.
From (ii): *People used to believe that* having a red ear *meant* that somebody *was* talking about them.

Exercise 3
Rewriting

There are many superstitions about cats. These are some of them. Complete each of the sentences after each paragraph to make sentences like those in Exercise 2. Use information from the paragraph to do so.

1 In ancient Egypt the cat was a goddess. The people made statues of cats, usually women with cat's heads. Women wanted to look like cats, with narrow eyes and a gentle walk. They never hurt cats. It was unlucky. The Persians knew this. So, when they attacked an Egyptian army once, they let cats run in front of the soldiers. The Egyptians did not fight!
The ancient Egyptians used to believe that .... and that ....
2 In Japan, some people bury cats in special temples. Japanese Buddhists believe this will bring them good luck.
Japanese Buddhists believe ....

3 The early Christians wanted to stop the worship of cats. They said that cats were the friends of the Devil. A person who owned a cat would be unlucky.
The early Christians wanted people to believe ....
4 In Scotland, at the end of the fifteenth century, the people believed that if they threw a cat into the sea, there would be a shipwreck. Two 'witches' were once burned for trying to do this while a King and a Queen were on a ship.
In Scotland, they used to believe that .... meant ....

5 In France, for several hundred years, 13 cats were burned every year. After burning the cats, they thought that there would be no illness. The King used to go to the ceremony. Louis XIV stopped this custom after 1648.
The French used to believe that .... meant ....

6 In America, people often say that if you let a cat come near a dead person, that person's family will have bad luck.
Some Americans say that .... is .... for the dead person's family.

7 In Holland they say that if you dislike cats you will need an umbrella at your wedding (ie it will rain).
The Dutch say that .... means ....

8 The Burmese believe that anyone who has a white cat will be very lucky. During the Second World War the people in Burma refused to help the British Army until they painted white cats on their tanks, cars, etc.
The Burmese think that .... is ....

9 In Brittany (France) there is a superstition that every black cat has one perfect white hair, and that if you find it, pull it out, and keep it, you will have the best of luck in love or money.
Some French people believe that .... and that .... means ....

Exercise 4
Planned essay

Use the sentences in Exercise 3 as well as your own ideas to write an essay called '*Superstition*'. Follow this plan:

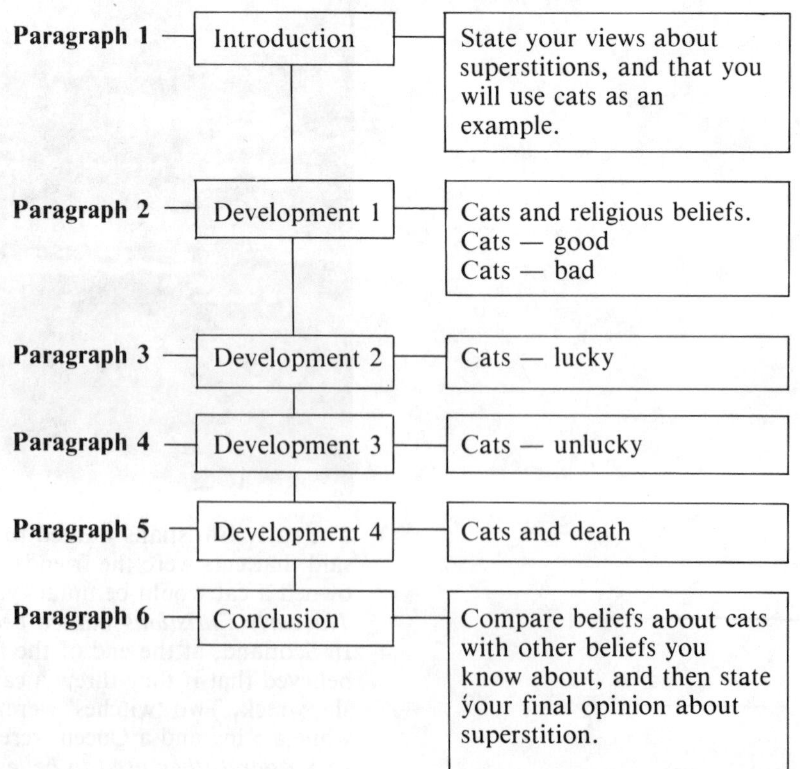

Exercise 5
Free writing

Use the information in these two surveys to write an essay called 'People need cats'.

Survey 1 People answered the question 'Why do you think people keep cats?' like this:

43% because of loneliness
26% to keep away mice and rats
21% because they like animals
19% as company for children
5% to make the home look comfortable

Survey 2 People answered these questions:

Do you think:	YES %	NO %	DON'T KNOW %
Your cat needs you	22	3	75
Cats understand people	73	24	3
Cats are nicer than people	13	40	47
Cats are good company	50	3	47
A cat shows its owner's character	57	25	18
Cats understand people's speech	41	54	5

Unit 17

Logical order for instructions

Comparing instructions with advice and warnings

Putting information together in a fluent essay

Exercise 1
Completion

Mrs Peters has asked her husband to do the washing while she is shopping. She has left him some instructions. Write them out, making a choice at the beginning of each sentence, and filling the blanks with one of the following: put, shut, turn, fill, press, press.

Then/First, ... the washing into the machine and .... the door tight. Then/In addition, ... the programme selector to Regular Wash 95°. Next/From time to time, ... the two soap trays with soap powder. Next/After that, — and very important — .... the button in the middle of the dial until the arrow points to PRE-WASH. Finally/In addition, ... the starter.

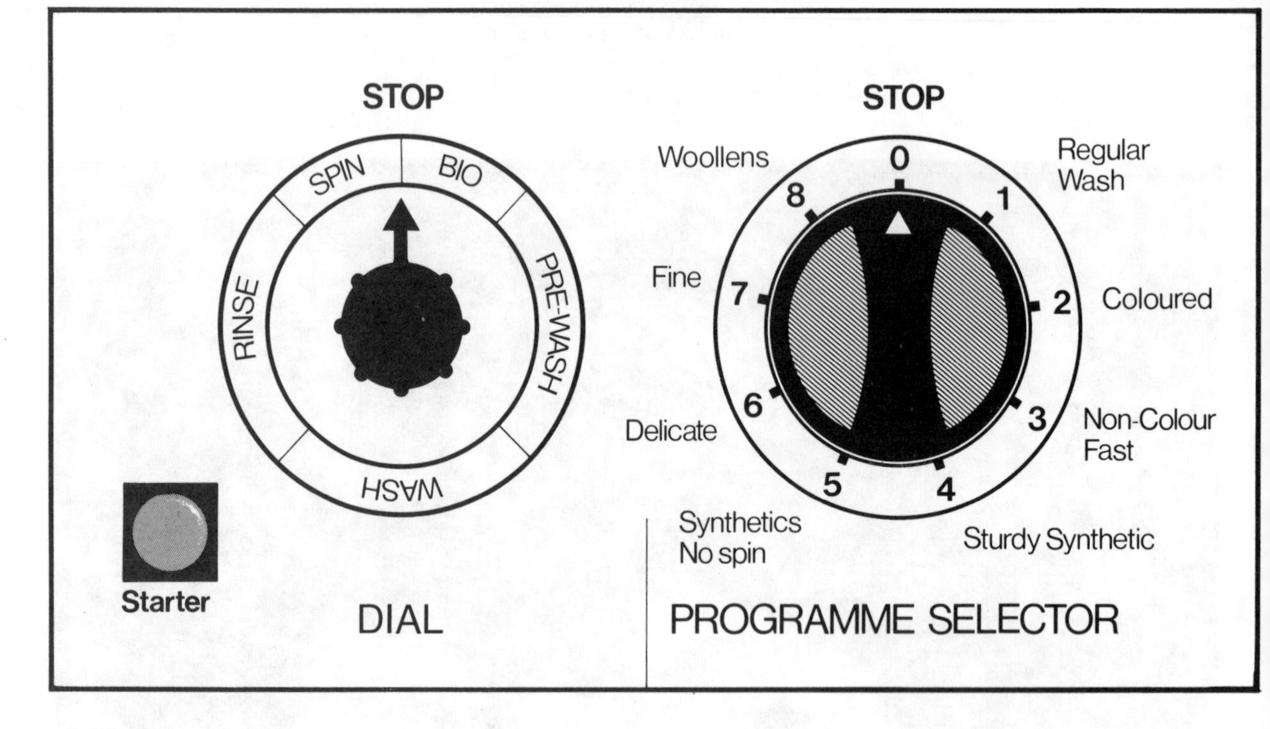

Exercise 2
Guided writing

Mrs Peters has a new cooker. She wants to bake a cake, but she doesn't understand how to use the OVEN TIMER. The instructions are too difficult. Look at the OVEN TIMER and the numbers for the different parts. These numbers show the order in which Mrs Peters has to use the parts. Write simple instructions similar to those in Exercise 1.
(*Note:* The labels on the drawing omit *the*.)

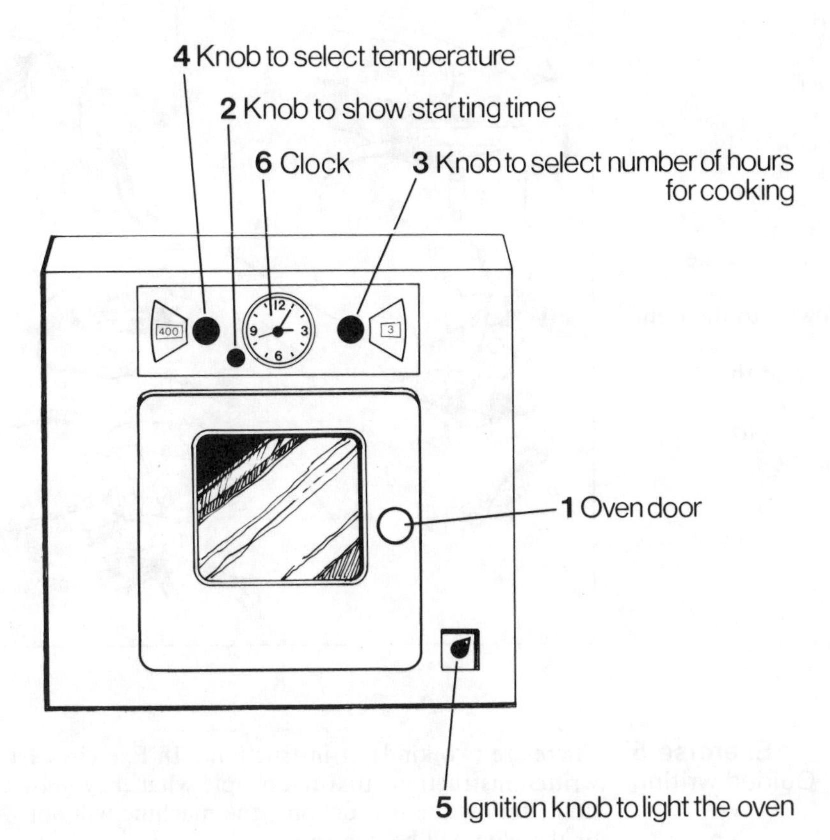

Exercise 3
Joining sentences

When there is an instruction to do two things at the same time, we can say:

Do the washing.
Use the machine. } Do the washing, *using* the machine.

(i) Match each sentence on the left with one sentence on the right. Then join each pair, making a sentence with .... *ing*.

Put the washing into the machine.	Press the starter.
Select the programme.	Use the soap trays.
Put soap powder into the machine.	Press the button in the middle.
Make the arrow point to PRE-WASH.	Shut the door tight.
Start the programme.	Turn the programme selector knob.

(ii) Look back at your instructions in Exercise 2. If there are any sentences you could join with .... ing like those in (i) above, change them.

Exercise 4
Ordering and joining sentences

Put these instructions in the right order and combine sentences (as in Exercise 3) wherever possible. The pictures will help you.

Wiring a Plug

Replace the cover.
Remove the case.
Use a screwdriver.
Screw it down tight.
Unscrew the screws.
Avoid damage to the wires.
Trim the plastic around the wires.
Join the brown wire to the right terminal.
Join the blue wire to the left terminal.
Join the striped wire to the earth terminal.

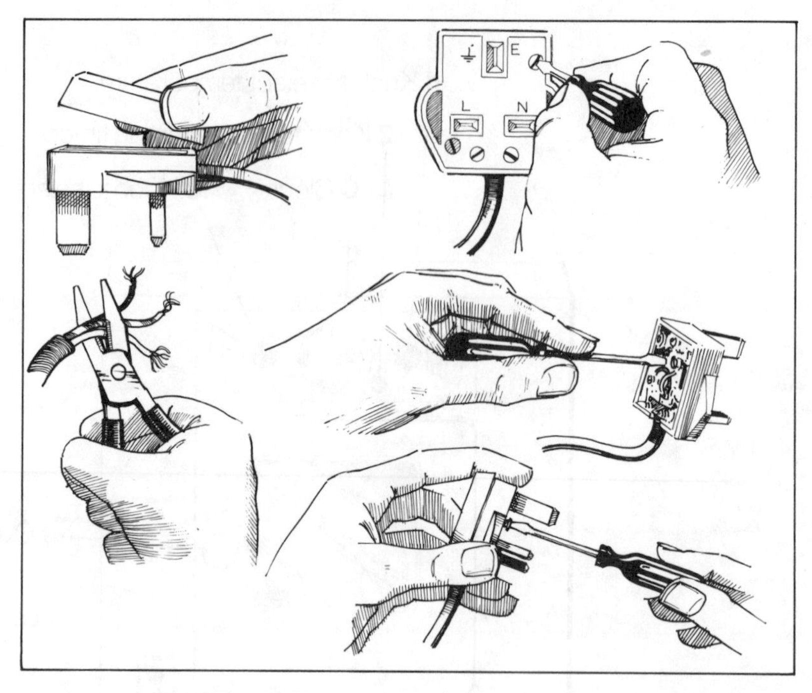

Exercise 5
Guided writing

There are two kinds of instructions. In Exercises 1 to 4, you have written instructions that tell people what they *must* do. If they don't follow the instructions, the machine will not work properly, or the plug will be dangerous.
There are also instructions that *advise* people about the *best* things to do or *warn* them of dangers. For instructions like these, we use expressions such as:

Advice:	It is a good idea to It is best to Make sure you Take care to Be sure to You should	take no risks. put the fire out properly.
Warning:	You should not Be careful not to Take care not to It is unwise to It is never a good idea to	spread the fire. take unnecessary risks.
	Avoid	spreading the fire.

Use the following information about how to put out fires, and write some instructions giving advice and warnings. Arrange your instructions according to the different things we can use.
Start with a paragraph about what to do if there is a fire.
Next, write separate paragraphs about using (i) water, earth or sand, (ii) blankets, and (iii) fire extinguishers. Write a final paragraph about special dangers.

Use as many of the advice and warning expressions as possible. Join sentences whenever possible, using *and, but, while, when, because* etc.

IF THERE IS A FIRE IN A ROOM:
Shut all the doors and windows if possible.
Leave the room and the building, if it is a big fire.
Stay and try to put the fire out if it is a small fire.
Telephone the fire brigade.
Warn other people.
Don't risk your life to save unnecessary things.
If you are trapped in a room with a fire, *crawl.*
Put a handkerchief around your mouth to keep the smoke out of your lungs.
If you have to break a window, don't use your hands.
If you have to jump, hang from the window before jumping.
When jumping, relax.
Don't use a lift in a burning building.

HOW TO PUT OUT A FIRE
Water is good for most fires.
But water is not for:
electrical fires, unless the electricity is turned *off,*
paraffin (kerosene) fires on a hard floor, though water is useful if the paraffin is burning on a carpet,
burning fat.

Earth or sand is good for small fires.
Earth or sand is not good for burning oil or fat.

A blanket or overcoat is good for small fires.
Wrap a blanket or overcoat around a person whose clothes are burning.
Use a blanket or overcoat on a burning TV.
Do not use a blanket or overcoat for a large fire, because they will burn as well.

A fire blanket is a special blanket made for fires. It is often made of glass fibre.
It is good for people whose clothes are burning.
It is also good for small fires.
If fat is burning on the cooker, use a fire blanket.
Protect your hands from the flames. The blanket should have handles on the back to protect your hands.

There are many kinds of fire extinguishers.
If you have one, learn how to use it.
Don't use a fire extinguisher on burning fat.

SPECIAL DANGERS
Don't pick up something burning.
Don't carry something burning out of a door. The air will blow the flames back onto you.
Don't throw water or sand onto burning fat. There will be a rain of burning fat all over you.
If you (or another person) are burning, rolling on the floor is best.
Cover another person in a blanket. Don't let them run around.

Unit 18

Definition

Information from graphs

Classifying information

Narrative about past events

Phrases for introducing and concluding essays, for disagreeing, and for supporting a viewpoint

In this unit you will write an essay on *Mechanisation and Human Life*. People are worried because machines, especially robots, take away their jobs.

Exercise 1
Introducing an essay

First, we must write the Introduction, in one paragraph. There are many ways of introducing an essay. These are a few of the main ways:

(i) *A definition of the topic.* For this essay, you could define mechanisation. Here is an example of a definition.

Industrialisation means building factories to make the things that people need. Industrialisation can affect agriculture, ancient crafts and trades (eg pottery, shoe-making), and influence where people live (since they have to live near the factories, usually in the cities).

Complete this definition of *mechanisation:* (Look at the MECHANISATION CHART on page 65.) You will need words like: *work, means, power, tool, control, human, mechanised.*

Mechanisation means making .... to do the .... that was done by .... before that time. In mechanisation, it could be the ...., or the ...., or the .... that is .... -ed. Machines that provide the ...., the ...., and the ...., and do not need .... at all, are called ....

(ii) *A question that the essay will answer* eg 'Will robots spoil our lives?' Think of two more questions for this topic.

(iii) *Some useful statistics* Here are three graphs. Use them to write three sentences about the increasing number of electronic computers, robots, and industrial microcomputers in the world.

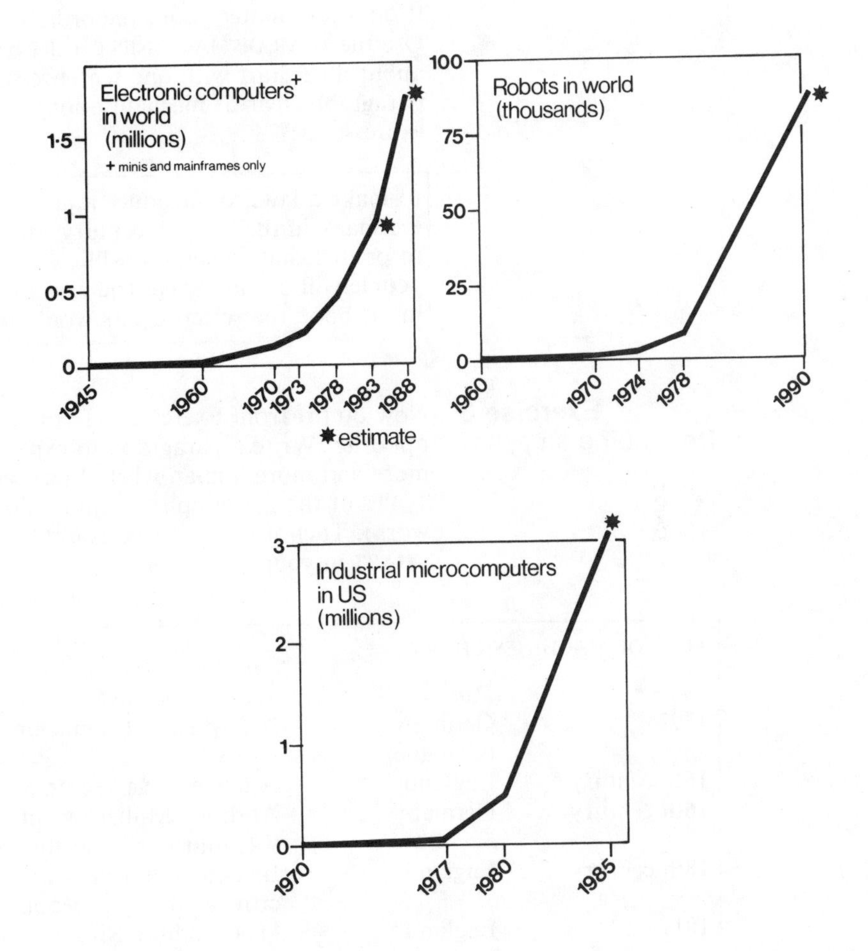

(iv) *Personal experience* eg a brief story (two or three sentences) about how you (or somebody you know or imagine) lost a job because of a new machine.
Write such a brief story.

Now write the introduction (one paragraph) for your essay. You can use all four openings above if you wish, in any order you like. Or else you can use one, two, or three of these openings.

You might need expressions like:

a serious problem; unemployment (= no jobs); quality of life; the need to work; in the first place; let us define . . . .; it is useful to define . . . .; we can ask ourselves . . . .; some important facts . . . .; a brief story will illustrate the problem; will affect everybody

Exercise 2
Developing an essay

In the next part of the essay, we can do two things:

(i) We can give some examples of people's fear of mechanisation.

(ii) We can classify (describe in a clear way) the different kinds of mechanisation, and explain briefly the history of mechanisation.
It does not matter about the order of (i) and (ii). Let us do (i) first. Use the FEAR OF MACHINES CHART below to write one paragraph about this. Start with one sentence stating the TOPIC of the paragraph (fear of mechanisation). You may need these expressions:

> to make a law; to introduce a law; in .... th century England/ Germany in the .... th century; there were riots; to do a survey; to predict that something will .... (eg Mr Brown predicts that people will use many electric cars by 1990; or: Mr Brown predicted in his book that electric cars would be common by 1990.)

Exercise 3
Developing an essay

Now do (ii) from Exercise 2. Look at the MECHANISATION CHART opposite. Write a paragraph to explain how machines started to do more and more human work. Start with one sentence giving the TOPIC of the paragraph (machines do more and more human work). Then use about five examples from the MECHANISATION CHART in your paragraph.

FEAR OF MACHINES CHART

Date	*Place*	*What happened*
1397	Germany (Cologne)	A law against a machine for making pins
16th century	England	A law against factories for weaving material
16th century	Germany	Anthony Müller invented a machine to spin cloth. He was murdered and the machine was destroyed.
18th century	England	Inventors and their machines were often attacked by crowds of angry people.
1811 – 12	England	'The Luddite Riots' — angry crowds destroyed 1100 machines that made materials.
1939	USA	A survey of people's opinions (Gallup Poll) blamed machines for unemployment.
1950	USA	A survey asked people what they feared most. The greatest fear was war. Next was automation (= the use of machines).
1980	International Labour Office	J. Rada in *The Impact of Microelectronics* writes that there will be fewer jobs in the future. Even if the working day ends earlier, and even if new factories are built, there will be fewer jobs because robots will do most of the work.

MECHANISATION CHART

	WORK	COUNTRY	DATE	POWER	TOOL	CONTROL
Human work	Walking	—	2.5M BC	Human Body	Legs	Human Brain
	Handwriting	Egypt	3500 BC	Human Body	Hands	Human Brain
	Hand weaving	Egypt	3500 BC	Human Body	Hands	Human Brain
Work helped by power from nature	Sail boat	Egypt	3300 BC	Wind	Boat	Human Brain
	Water mill	Greece	85 BC	Water	Grindstone	"
	Wind mill	Persia	664	Wind	Grindstone	"
	Spinning	UK	1769	Water	Wheels etc	"
Work helped by animals or tools	Ox plough	Meso-potamia	3000 BC	Animal	Plough	Human Brain
	Cutting wheel	Unknown	3000 BC	Human Body	Cutting edge	"
	Horse and cart	Meso-potamia	2500 BC	Animal	Wheel	"
	Spinning wheel	India	c. 1000	Human Body	Wheel	"
	Typewriter	US	1867	Human Body	Typeface	"
Work helped by machines, but human brain in control	Steam train	UK	1829	Steam engine	Wheel	Human Brain
	Car	Germany	1885	Engine	Wheel	"
	Aeroplane	US	1903	Engine	Propeller	"
	Flour mill	US	1785	Engine	Conveyor	Machine/brain
	Biscuit-making	UK	1830	Engine	Conveyor	Machine/brain
	Meat packing	US	1880	Engine	Conveyor	Machine/brain
	Assembly line	US	1913	Electricity	Conveyor	Machine/brain
Work done completely by machines, but humans still needed	Clock	Europe	c. 1300	Clock work	Mechanical hands	Machine
	Pressure cooker	France	1680	Open fire	Steam	Machine
	Steam pump	UK	1705	Steam engine	Pump	Machine
	Jacquard loom	France	1801	Steam engine	Pump	Machine
	Making tools	US	1860	Electric motor	Cutting tool	Machine
	Typewriter	US	1960	Electric motor	Typeface	Machine
Work done by robots (humans not needed)	Machine tool	US	1960	Electric motor	Cutting machine	Computer
	Robot	US	c. 1960	Electric motor	Mechanical hands	Computer
	Robot with vision	UK	1980	Electric motor	Mechanical hands	Computer

Exercise 4
Developing an essay

In Exercises 1, 2 and 3, you wrote the main part of your essay.

Now you need a final paragraph, a conclusion. There are several ways you can write it:

(i) If you did not use all four openings in your first, introductory, paragraph, you can use one or more of those four as a conclusion.

(ii) You can write a summary of the whole essay. You may need some of these expressions:

in conclusion; to summarise; the main facts are ....; to sum up; in short; the main facts about .... are ....; the main point is that ....

(iii) You can just give your opinion about mechanisation, eg ask the question 'Do we need to be afraid of mechanisation?' and then give your answer.

Write your concluding paragraph using (i), (ii) or (iii).

Exercise 5
Free writing

You have written an essay in four paragraphs about *Mechanisation and Human Life* which emphasises people's fear of mechanisation. Exchange essays with another student.

Imagine that you read this essay in a newspaper or magazine, and that you do *not* think people should fear machines or robots. You think that mechanisation will *improve* human life.

Write a short letter (one or two paragraphs) to the newspaper or magazine saying what you disagree with, and why you disagree.

You may need these expressions:

> I would like to comment on ....; the essay on .... was very interesting but I ....; there are several points I cannot accept; on the other hand; the writer ignores the fact that ....; we must remember that ....; one advantage of mechanisation is ....; another is ....; there are numerous arguments for mechanisation; I would like to emphasise that ....; moreover; do not forget that ....

Unit 19

Presenting an argument; arguing against a case

Logical arrangement in arguments

Language of persuasion

In this unit you are going to prepare a debate (an argument between two teams) about the statement:

Most unhappiness in the world is caused by people.

In a debate there are two teams. One team agrees with the statement. The other team disagrees. In this debate, the side which disagrees must argue that:

Most unhappiness in the world is not caused by people but by nature, eg death, illness, storms, etc. *or by events that people cannot control*, eg economics, industry, population growth, etc.

Each team has two speakers. One speaker presents the arguments for his team. The other speaker argues against each argument that the opposite team has presented.

The class should divide into two teams, one for each side of the debate. Each team works as a group and prepares a speech, which one person from the team will read aloud to the whole class (or, if possible, to another class in the school).

Exercises 1–4 help to prepare the speeches for the first speaker of each team.

Exercise 1
Planning a speech
TEAM 1 ONLY

(i) First write a list of how people can make themselves or others unhappy. These are a few ideas: ambition, anger, greed, hate, intolerance, jealousy, love of money, love of power, meanness, lack of pity, lack of kindness, lack of equality. Try to add more to this list.

(ii) Now try to arrange your list in groups like this:

human emotions	*lack of feeling*	*actions*	*faults in society*
hate, greed, etc.	lack of pity, etc.	stealing, cruelty, etc.	lack of equality, lack of medicine, etc.

Add any more columns that you need.

(iii) Now, go down each column and note examples to prove your argument. You may use a true event (perhaps from your own life), or one from a famous story, or from history.

Exercise 2
Writing a speech
TEAM 1 ONLY

Write one paragraph for each column, with examples, from Exercise 1 (ii) and (iii).

You may need these expressions:

sometimes very often usually	....	cause(s) is/are the cause of results(s) in	some a lot of a great deal of	unhappiness misery problems

We know that	most many	people are . . . .

We often see people who . . . .
Everyone here must know somebody who . . . .
You have all heard of . . . . in the book . . . . by . . . . (author).
This is an example of . . . .

This These	example(s) show	that . . . . how . . . .

Exercise 3
Writing an introduction
TEAM 1 ONLY

What you wrote in Exercise 2 is the main part of your speech. Now you can write an introductory paragraph. It should state your main viewpoint and then *summarise* what you are going to say next (ie the examples you described in Exercise 2).

You might need some of these expressions in your introduction:

> it is absolutely certain that . . . .; we are quite sure that . . . .; there is no doubt at all that . . . .; I will explain how . . . .; I will convince you that . . . .; you will agree with me that . . . .; the most important causes of . . . . are . . . .; the main reasons for . . . . are . . . .; . . . . is caused by . . . .;

Exercise 4
Writing conclusion
TEAM 1 ONLY

Finally, write a conclusion in one paragraph. You might use some of these expressions:

> Now I am sure it is clear to you that . . . .
> You cannot doubt that . . . .
> These examples have convinced you, I am sure, that . . . .
> Of course you now agree with me about . . . .
> I have shown you that . . . .
> I have given you examples of how . . . .
> The examples I gave have convinced you, I am sure, that . . . .

Exercise 1
Planning a speech
TEAM 2 ONLY

(i) First make a list of how nature or events that we cannot control may make us unhappy.

(ii) Then try to arrange your list in groups like this:

death	*illness*	*nature* *storm* etc	*events that people cannot control* *economics*	*population* etc
of a loved person	self family	destroying home	lack of money lack of good homes lack of education	shortage of food shortage of doctors

Add any more columns that you need.

(iii) Now, go down each column and note examples to prove your argument. See also the Exercise 1 instruction for Team 1.

Exercise 2
Writing a speech
TEAM 2 ONLY

As for Team 1
You may need these expressions also:

We have all heard of events like the death of a . . .
a sudden flood
a train crash
Many events can cause . . . .
Everyone here knows that lack of money can cause . . . .
hunger

Exercise 3
Writing an introduction
TEAM 2 ONLY

As for Team 1

Exercise 4
Writing a conclusion
TEAM 2 ONLY

As for Team 1

Exercise 5
Free writing

When each team has finished the speech, they give it to the other team. Each team writes a reply to argue against each point in the other team's speech. The reply should follow the order of the first speech.

You may need these expressions:

The opposing team has argued that ....
We have heard the arguments for the view that ....
My opponent has said that ....
We cannot accept their argument that ....
It is impossible to agree that ....
No one could believe that ....
That is a false argument because ....
The argument is nonsense because ....
since ....
But, on the other hand, ...
If you agree that .... then you will also agree that ....

The teams keep their reply secret until the debate.

THE DEBATE

The speeches are given in this order:

Team 1, Speaker 1.
Team 2, Speaker 1.
Team 1, Speaker 2 (arguing against Team 2, Speaker 1).
Team 2, Speaker 2 (arguing against Team 1, Speaker 1).

There should be a judge, perhaps the teacher, or a group of judges (perhaps the whole class, or another class in the same school). The judge(s) award points to each speaker:

1 point for every good argument.
2 points for every *very* good argument.

The team with the greatest number of points wins the debate.

Unit 20

Describing activities

Making suggestions

Historical narrative

In this unit you will prepare a tourist brochure to attract visitors to your own town. It will consist of one page in four sections.

Exercise 1
Guided writing

First write a paragraph about the principal attractions — the most important places to visit. Three or four might be enough.

Start your paragraph with a sentence listing them.

There are .... (number) of { attractions in .... They are .... / interesting sights in ....

or

The .... (number) { principal attractions in .... are .... / interesting sights in .... are ....

Then describe each one briefly, like this: use one sentence to say what the *location* and the *function* are. Then use a second sentence to mention a *special point*. These are two examples:

The beautiful Star Fountain [LOCATION] faces Central Square and is admired for the star-shaped patterns it makes [FUNCTION]. People throw coins into it for good luck [SPECIAL POINT].

In the south-east quarter [LOCATION] is the Old Town Hall which is used for [FUNCTION] all important public ceremonies in the town. You should look at its painted ceiling [SPECIAL POINT].

Exercise 2
Guided writing

Next, write a paragraph about the principal things to do in the town. Three or four interesting activities might be enough. Start this paragraph with a sentence listing them.

You can spend a	busy interesting etc.	week day month etc.	enjoy*ing* try- visit- etc.	and .... and ...., and learn*ing* our .... use- watch-

Then describe each activity briefly. Say what the activity is and where it is. These are two examples:

You will enjoy a ride in the London underground which has nearly 300 stations in the centre and right across the city.
There are especially good Chinese restaurants in London, mostly in Chinatown not far from Piccadilly Circus.

Some more activities are: a ride in a tram, an overhead railway, a cable car, a horse-drawn carriage; visiting a nightclub; sports like golf, water-skiing, ice-skating, fishing, etc; going to the theatre; attending concerts; etc.

Exercise 3
Guided writing

Now you can give a brief history of the city. The main kinds of information you could give are:
(i) How old is it?
(ii) Who founded it?
(iii) Who were its famous citizens?
Your third paragraph could start:

This is a(n) { ancient / new / re-built } city. It was founded in .... (year) by .... (people)

Continue the third paragraph with a few important details from the history of the city.
Your fourth paragraph could give some information about a few (maybe two or three) interesting people in the history of the city. Tell:
(i) Their names
(ii) The time (approximately) when they lived
(iii) Why they are famous: what they did
(iv) Any statues or other ways of remembering them (eg street names).

Exercise 4
Free writing

Finally, describe two interesting facts about your city. For example:
a How you celebrate a birthday, or a wedding, or a historic date;
b How you elect your leaders;
c How the education is organised.
Write two paragraphs, one about each interesting fact you choose.

Exercise 5
Group writing

Join in a group with four or five other students and read each other's work. Put all the information together to make one long tourist brochure including all the facts from each person's writing.